Building Blocks of the Faith

D0981605

Building Blocks of the Faith
Foundational Bible Doctrines

*A Thirteen Week
Sunday School Curriculum Series*

Editorial Committee

Dr. Truman Dollar
Dr. Jerry Falwell
Dr. A. V. Henderson
Dr. Jack Hyles

Fundamentalist Church Publications
Nashville, Tennessee

Copyright © 1977 by Fundamentalist Church Publications. All rights reserved under International and Pan-American Conventions. Published by Fundamentalist Church Publications, P.O. Box 24520, Nashville, Tennessee 37202. Manufactured in the United States of America.

Permission is granted to the purchaser to reproduce the Study Worksheets included in each chapter for distribution to Sunday school students only. Reproduction or distribution of any other portion of this book without written permission is strictly forbidden.

ISBN 0-8407-3025-X

Table of Contents

Statement
of Purpose

Sunday school material for Bible-believing, Fundamentalist churches is the major goal of Fundamentalist Church Publications. Each member of the Editorial Committee is an experienced pastor. Each one has faced the challenge of providing his Sunday school teachers with both solidly biblical material and useful study tools for preparing weekly lessons. This curriculum series is designed to meet that challenge with a doctrinally sound, highly practical, and uniquely flexible program of lessons and reinforcement materials.

As great as the need is for trustworthy curriculum material, the members of the Editorial Committee have yet another goal for Fundamentalist Church Publications—a demonstration of unity among brothers in Christ. Fundamentalists are solidly in agreement on the foundational doctrines of the Bible. They love Christ, hate sin, trust the Word of God, and win souls. The members of the Editorial Committee are seeking to encourage Fundamentalists, by their own example, to cooperate with one another in the task of reaching the world for Jesus Christ. "Can two walk together, except they be agreed?" (Amos 3:3). Of course not. But when two are in agreement, there can be walking together and working together. Fundamentalist Church Publications is aiming to create a spirit of agreement among Fundamentalists so that there can be a united front in the fight against wickedness.

The Editors

"Having seen that there was a great need for Sunday school helps in Fundamental churches, we have committed ourselves to the long term project of producing these materials. We reviewed and discarded several approaches to the need before arriving at a format we feel is best adapted to Fundamental churches."

Dr. Truman Dollar is pastor of the Kansas City Baptist Temple in Kansas City, Missouri. Under his ministry, Baptist Temple has consistently ranked among America's fastest growing congregations. He is author of the book "How to Carry Out God's Stewardship Plan", now in its second printing, and is nationally recognized as a speaker and authority on church finances. Dr. Dollar is a founder and vice-president of Baptist Bible College East, Peekskill, New York. He attended Baptist Bible College, Springfield, Missouri, and is a graduate of the University of Missouri.

"Fundamentalist Sunday schools have always been Bible Sunday schools. We are not offering a series of booklets to replace direct Bible teaching. Instead, we offer a high quality study guide that will help teachers and pastors dig deeper into the riches of God's Word."

Dr. Jerry Falwell is pastor of the Thomas Road Baptist Church, Lynchburg, Virginia. He organized the church in 1956 with 35 charter members. It now has a membership of approximately 14,000. Dr. Falwell is best known as director of The Old Time Gospel Hour, a nationally syndicated television broadcast of the weekly services of the Thomas Road church. In 1971 Dr. Falwell founded Liberty Baptist College, of which he is chancellor. Dr. Falwell attended Lynchburg College and is a graduate of Baptist Bible College, Springfield, Missouri.

"We sincerely believe that working together to provide materials that Fundamentalists can trust will tend to promote unity among Bible-believing people that is sorely needed."

Dr. A. V. Henderson is pastor of the Temple Baptist Church, Detroit, Michigan. He is a former president of Baptist Bible Fellowship International and has held pastorates in Texas, Delaware, and Michigan. Dr. Henderson is a founder and president of Baptist Bible College East, Peekskill, New York. He attended Wayland College, Plainview, Texas, and holds honorary degrees from Baptist Bible College, Springfield, Missouri, and California Graduate School of Theology.

"Fundamentalist Church Publications fills a void that has been present in Fundamental circles for years. I rejoice in its birth and will do my utmost to perpetuate its life."

Dr. Jack Hyles is pastor of the First Baptist Church, Hammond, Indiana. Under his leadership the First Baptist Sunday school has grown to be the largest in the world. His annual week-long pastors' school draws thousands of pastors from all areas of the country. He is in constant demand as a speaker, particularly to groups of preachers, and is the author of a number of books. He is founder and president of Hyles-Anderson College. Dr. Hyles attended North Texas Agricultural College and East Texas Baptist College and holds an honorary degree from Bob Jones University.

Foundational Bible Doctrines

INTRODUCTION

This lesson series was produced entirely by God-fearing, Bible-believing pastors. These are men who not only believe God's Word, but have successfully applied it on the field. In their writing, they have not been bound by any confining rule or convention. Instead, they have written, as God has lead them, materials which are both fundamental in content and flexible in application.

The lessons in this series are doctrinally sound and can be taught with confidence. The illustrations and projects which comprise the reinforcement materials are flexible, allowing the individual teacher to use as many, or as few, as are appropriate.

No house can stand without a foundation. Jesus said that everyone who heard His words and obeyed them was like a wise man building his house on a rock. Peter spoke of Chistians as a spiritual house, built of living stones. Paul wrote of a foundation in Christ. The New Testament is filled with the command to edify the brethren in Christ, and the word edify, itself, means to build. The process of building is an illustration called on frequently by biblical writers.

Christian maturity doesn't just happen. It is a building process. The goal of this lesson series—Building Blocks of the Faith, Foundational Bible Doctrines—is to provide pastors and Sunday school teachers with the materials they need to begin that process of building up the brethren in the most holy faith. While preparing these lessons, we must keep in mind that we are not theologians teaching a seminary class. We are dedicated Sunday school teachers trying to show lay people, especially children and young people, the importance that Bible doctrines should play in their lives. We must remember that the greatest teacher of all cloaked His profundity in simplicity, and that which is profound can only be transferred from one mind to another in the vehicle of simplicity. For this reason, we will not go into the intricacies of every doctrine, nor will we explore some of their depths. And though we will pause briefly to be tantalized, we will, nevertheless, simply pause, look, be tempted, and pass by on the other side. We must be continually reminded that the presentation of God's Word must be clear and precise. It was after hearing the great C. H. Spurgeon that a young 10-year-old boy turned to his mother and said, "He isn't such a great preacher. I understood everything he said." When told of this statement, Spurgeon replied, "Would to God that every sermon I preach may be clearly understood by a 10-year-old lad." It was Spurgeon himself who continually reminded his students that "God has called you to feed the sheep, not the giraffes." When the food is so high that only the giraffes can reach it, the sheep will die of starvation. It is not our purpose to teach the complexities of Bible doctrines but to clearly present the wonders of these truths as the foundation for our belief.

These lessons are not to be considered crutches for the spiritually crippled, but tools for the spiritually active. Each pastor and teacher should carefully read every point, carefully study every Scripture reference, and prayerfully consider every illustration or project. Developing spiritual maturity in Sunday school students is a building process. This series contains the building blocks that will, when properly placed, provide a sure foundation for a fulfilling Christian life.

Guide to Creative Study

This book has been designed to encourage creative study and presentation of the Sunday school lesson by teachers to all age levels. Here are some of the unique features this lesson series offers:

1. References for Study—A complete list of all Scripture references used in each lesson. This makes it possible for the teacher to completely familiarize himself with every Bible verse used in the lesson before beginning study of the actual outline.

2. Point of Action—An attention getting illustration, project, or demonstration that quickly draws the student into the subject matter of each lesson.

3. Reinforcing Illustrations—Projects, stories, applications, and object lessons that allow each teacher to adapt the lesson material to his own class, regardless of the age level or number of students.

4. Craft Projects—Simple things to make and do that creatively illustrate to younger pupils the truths taught in each lesson.

5. Student Study Worksheets—A simple, yet effective device to encourage the pupils to take notes during the teaching time. Not a test, this fill-in-the-blank study sheet requires the individual students to listen for the major points of the lesson and write them in the appropriate spaces as the teacher presents them. These sheets should be reproduced and distributed to the students before class begins.

6. Teacher's Study Worksheet—A flexible study tool and visual aid, this page is not merely a master copy of the answers for the Student sheet. This page has several important uses. It may be reproduced on overhead projection transparencies. The contents can be used on chalkboard or charts to give visual reinforcement to the lesson—while it is being taught! Finally, this page gives the major points of the lesson at a glance, allowing the teacher to "zero in" on the areas of emphasis.

7. Wide Margins—A special feature that allows the teacher to mark areas for emphasis and add illustrations and material from personal sources.

FOUNDATIONAL BIBLE DOCTRINES

Truman Dollar, Pastor, Kansas City Baptist Temple
Kansas City, Missouri

Lesson One—Inspiration of Scripture

INTRODUCTION.
  I. WE NEED AN INSPIRED BIBLE.
    A. God is Greater than Man.
    B. Man is Separated from God.
    C. Sin has Severe Consequences.
  II. WHAT IS INSPIRATION?
    A. Theopneustos—God Breathed.
    B. Pheromai—Borne Along.
    C. Verbal-Plenary Inspiration.
  III. WHAT IS THE EVIDENCE OF AN INSPIRED BIBLE?
    A. Scriptural Unity is Miraculous.
    B. Bible Prophecy is Completely Accurate.
    C. Archaeology Confirms Scripture.
    D. The Bible is Historically Accurate.
CONCLUSION.

References for Study:
   Gen. 3; 9:26; 22:18; 26:4; 28:14; 49:10; 2 Sam. 7:12–16; Ps. 16:10; 22; 30:3–9; 34:20; 40:1, 2; 69:21; Is. 7:14; 40:3; 53:10; 55:9; Jer. 17:9; Dan. 2:37–45; 9:24–26; Hos. 6:2; Mic. 5:2; Zech. 9:9,10; 12:10; Luke 24:25–27; John 6:44; Rom. 1:17–25; 3:23; 2 Cor. 4:3,4; 2 Tim. 3:16; 2 Pet. 1:21.

Memory Verse:
   All scripture is given by inspiration of God, and is profitable for doctrine, for reproof, for correction, for instruction in righteousness: (2 Tim. 3:16).

Aim:
   To show that the Bible is the perfect and inspired Word of God.

Point of Contact:
   Lead the class (or a selected group within the class) in a round of the game Gossip. Whisper a brief phrase in the ear of the first student. He should then whisper the message to the next student, and so on, until the message has been repeated to everyone. What the last student hears will often be very different from the original statement. Write another message on a slip of paper. Give it to the first student with instructions to read the

message and then to pass the written message on. This message will stay the same, no matter how many people read it, because it was written down.

INTRODUCTION.

Inspire means to breathe in. Inspiration is the act of breathing in. When we speak of prompting something written or spoken, we refer to that prompting as inspiration. The Bible was written by men supernaturally inspired as they were moved by the Holy Spirit, so that their writings were complete, given word by word, and free from all error as no other writings ever have been or ever will be. The Bible is the Word of God. The Holy Spirit superintended the writers so as to influence even their very choice of words. The work of these holy men of old, under the guidance of the Holy Spirit, was so accurate that Jesus gave absolute endorsement to it, and so complete that we are forbidden to add to or take from it.

I. WE NEED AN INSPIRED BIBLE.

The inspiration of Scripture is a central theme among all Fundamentalists. But, why? Why do we believe in and need an inspired Bible? Because:

A. God is Greater than Man.

God is infinitely above mankind: His thoughts are above man's understanding (Is. 55:9). Only God can bridge this communication gap, and He has done it by revealing Himself in Scripture.

B. Man is Separated from God by Sin.

When man sinned in the Garden of Eden, his sin drove him from God's presence. He became spiritually dead (Gen. 3). He was no longer acceptable (Rom. 3:23). Man's sin separated him from God. If the two were to commune again, God would have to first communicate with man.

C. Man's Sin has Severe Consequences.

Man's fall into sin severely damaged those tools which he might use to communicate with God.

Man's heart was corrupted. It was defiled. It fell from innocence to deceitful wickedness (Jer. 17:9).

Man's intelligence was blighted. He was cast from the light of God's guidance to the darkness of sin. His mind was blinded to God's truth (2 Cor. 4:3,4).

Man's will was affected. He was distorted. He could no longer approach God on his own, nor could he even desire to (John 6:44).

Man's conscience was dulled. He saw no wrong in turning

from righteousness to unrighteousness. He no longer cared about good and evil (Rom. 1:17–25).

II. WHAT IS INSPIRATION?

The revelation of God to man came by means of inspiration. There are two Greek words that describe inspiration. The first is theopneustos (theo-news-tas). This is the word translated "inspiration" in 2 Tim. 3:16. The other key word is pheromai (fair-o-my). This word is translated "moved" in 2 Pet. 1:21.

A. The First Key Word is Theopneustos, or "God Breathed."

This Greek word applies to that which is written, not to the writers. It is not so much that the writers were inspired, but that their actual message or written words themselves were given by God.

B. A Second Key Word is Pheromai, or "Borne Along."

2 Pet. 1:21 tells us that holy men of old did not speak of their own interpretation but spoke and wrote as they were moved (pheromai—"picked up and carried about or borne along") by the Holy Spirit. It is the same word the Greeks would use to describe a sailing vessel borne along by the winds. This is God's movement in the writing of Scripture.

C. Verbal-Plenary Inspiration.

The Bible can best be described as given by verbal-plenary inspiration. The word *verbal* means that the very words that were written down were superintended by the Lord. *Plenary* means that inspiration was full or complete and extends to all the Bible, not just a part. All Scripture is God breathed, or given by inspiration.

III. WHAT IS THE EVIDENCE OF AN INSPIRED BIBLE?

A. Scriptural Unity is Miraculous.

There is no document, ancient or modern, that shows such unity and diversity as the Bible. This book was written over a period of about 1,600 years by more than 40 separate, human authors writing about the ultimate issues of life. Yet, there is not a single contradiction. This is clearly miraculous.

There are many indications of scriptural unity in the redemptive themes, covenants, sacrifices, and prophetic promises. Jesus said that there was unity in the Old Testament when he rebuked the Emmaus disciples in Luke 24:25–27. He called them blind for not seeing that the Old Testament had written concerning Him. He preached the messianic hope from Moses and the prophets.

The Old Testament writers prophesied the New Testament hope of redemption. The New Testament writers based much of

15

their gospel message on Old Testament prophecies. There is unity in Scripture.

B. Bible Prophecy is Completely Accurate.

Fulfilled prophecy is a convincing testimony to the divine origin of Scripture. The prophecies of the Bible always come true. The very nature of biblical prophecy demands a one hundred percent fulfillment record. There are literally hundreds of fulfilled Bible prophecies, but to illustrate the accuracy of God's prophetic passage, consider these two.

Prophecies concerning the sequence of the ancient empires have been fulfilled (Dan. 2:37–45): Nebuchadnezzar's Babylonian Empire, Medo-Persian Empire, Greek Empire of Alexander the Great, Roman Empire, and the split of the Roman Empire between the East and West. All of these empires are found in the prophecy of Daniel and all of this occurred precisely as it was given by Daniel.

Messianic prophecies, those concerning the coming of Christ, have also been fulfilled. The lineage of the Messiah was prophesied to be through a human family (Gen. 3:15), through Shem (Gen. 9:26), Abraham (Gen. 22:18), Isaac (Gen. 26:4), Jacob (Gen. 28:14), Judah (Gen. 49:10), and David (2 Sam. 7:12–16).

As to the Messiah's life, He was to have a virgin birth (Is. 7:14). His birthplace was to be in Bethlehem (Mic. 5:2). His forerunner would be John the Baptist (Is. 40:3). He would have a triumphal entry into Jerusalem (Zech. 9:9,10). He would come in a certain period of time according to the prophecy of Dan. 9:24–26.

At the Messiah's death, His side would be pierced (Zech. 12:10). He would have vinegar (Ps. 69:21). He would be mocked (Ps. 22:6–8). He would be naked (Ps. 22:17). His robe would be gambled over (Ps. 22:18). Not a bone would be broken (Ps. 34:20). There would be a great cry from the Cross (Ps. 22:1). He would have a broken heart (Ps. 22:14).

Prophecies concerning the Messiah's resurrection (Ps. 16:10; Hos. 6:2; Ps. 30:3, 9; Is. 53:10; Ps. 40:1, 2) all came to pass.

C. Archaeology Confirms Scripture.

A renowned Jewish archaeologist once wrote, "There may be stated categorically that no archaeological discovery has ever controverted a biblical reference." On the other hand, archaeology has frequently confirmed statements of the Bible. Cities once thought to be nonexistent by skeptical historians, were mentioned in the Bible. Many have been discovered by archaeologists.

Many kings and ruling potentates who were thought to be mythical characters have been found to be historical figures.

Archaeologists have discovered documents that support the Bible position.

D. *The Bible is Historically Accurate.*

History is confirmed by the Bible and the Bible is confirmed by history. The Scripture is true concerning historical events, although its primary purpose is not to describe the history of mankind. The Bible tells much about history. The known facts of history agree with the Scripture and Scripture with the known facts of history. Thousands of examples could be given to illustrate this point.

CONCLUSION.

The Bible is an infallible book, divinely inspired. It will never fail. This truth is the pole star to all other doctrines. It gives us a Bible we can trust and a final authority on all matters. The Bible is truth, and that which does not agree with the Bible is error.

Emphasize that the Bible is absolutely trustworthy. Encourage the students to read it and to live by its counsel.

Reinforcing Illustrations:

1. Put a Bible into a large envelope addressed to mankind. Tell the pupils that it is a letter from God. As the envelope is opened and the Bible removed, explain that just as the mailman delivers a letter from a person in another place, the writers of Scripture delivered to mankind a letter from God.

2. Select one pupil from the class, and give him a piece of paper and pencil. Read several passages of Scripture aloud, preferably 2 Tim. 3:16 and 2 Pet. 1:21, instructing the student to copy exactly what you are saying. When you are finished, ask him to stand and read the passages to the entire class—exactly as you gave them to him. This may not be a perfect illustration of the process of inspiration, but it will clearly illustrate that the Bible writers have given us exactly the words God wanted us to hear.

3. Bring a drawing, photo, or model of a sailing ship to class. Ask the students to explain how a sailing ship illustrates the doctrine of inspiration. Explain to them that a sailing ship is completely at the mercy of the wind. Ships have been known to sit dead in the water for days when they encountered a tropical calm. They can only move when there is wind. Likewise, the writers of Scripture could only produce when they were moved of the Holy Spirit. In using this illustration with older teens and adults, it may be helpful to explain that the Holy Spirit chose to use the same word to describe inspiration in 2 Pet. 1:21 that He chose to describe a ship driven by the wind in Acts 27:15–17.

4. Explain to the class that in seeking a job, a person is often asked for letters of reference or recommendation. The employer

will consider these recommendations before giving the applicant a job. We can do the same in deciding whether or not to accept the testimony of the Bible as reliable. Show the class four envelopes, representing letters of recommendation. Open and read these brief letters to the class. The first will recommend the Bible on the basis of its miraculous unity. The second will call to mind its fulfilled prophecy. The third will recall its archaeological confirmation. The fourth will speak of its historical accuracy. These four recommendations should conclusively establish the Bible as reliable. A variation of this illustration could be a mini-drama set in a courtroom. Four witnesses can be called before the judge to testify concerning the reliability of Scripture. They would, of course, be the same witnesses mentioned above. For this variation, scripts should be prepared in advance, though individual "actors" need not be chosen until the time when the drama is used.

Lesson One: Inspiration of Scripture
Lesson Text: 2 Tim. 3:16
Craft: A Bible
Materials Needed:
  Black and white construction paper
  Red grosgrain ribbon for markers
  Glue
  White ink
Instructions:
  In advance:
    Cut Bibles from the black construction paper.
    Cut white construction paper for inside pages.
    Cut the ribbon in correct lengths.
Have black and white paper folded, as for a book. Give one of each and a ribbon to the children. Let them glue the Bible together and insert the ribbon. When they are finished, write the memory verse in their "Bible". Write *Holy Bible* on the outside cover with white ink.

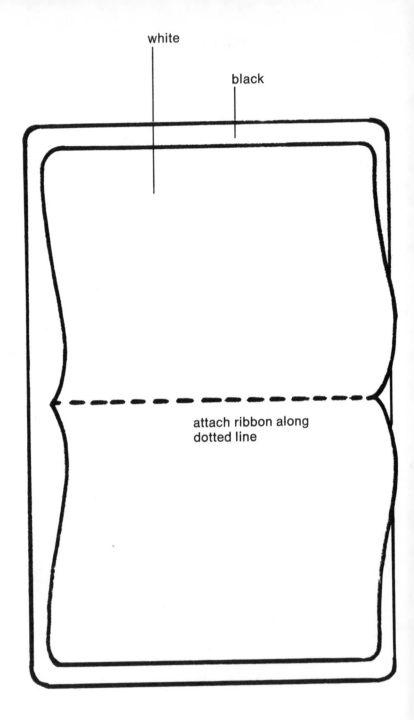

white

black

attach ribbon along
dotted line

STUDY WORKSHEET

Lesson One—INSPIRATION OF SCRIPTURE

WE NEED AN INSPIRED BIBLE.

1. God is _____.

    His _____ are above Man's _____(Isaiah 55:9).

2. Man is _____ from God by ____(Romans 3:23).

3. Sin has _____.

    Man's _____ has been _____(Jeremiah 17:9).

    Man's _____ has been _____(2 Corinthians 4:3,4).

    Man's _____ has been _____(John 6:44).

    Man's _____ has been _____(Romans 1:17–25).

WHAT IS INSPIRATION?

1. Two Key Words.

    a. Theopneustos means _____(2 Timothy 3:16).

    b. Pheromai means _____(2 Peter 1:21).

2. Biblical Position.

    a. Verbal—God inspired the _____.

    b. Plenary—Inspiration is _____.

EVIDENCE OF AN INSPIRED BIBLE.

1. Miraculous Unity.

    a. Written over _____ years.

    b. God used more than _____ authors.

    c. Covers ultimate issues of life, yet is without _____.

2. Accurate Prophecy.

    Prophetic passages spanning centuries have always proven

    to be _____.

3. Archaeological Confirmation.

    _____ discovery has repeatedly been confirmed

    by _____of the _____.

Memory Verse: All scripture is given by inspiration of God, and is profitable for doctrine, for reproof, for correction, for instruction in righteousness (2 Timothy 3:16).

Short Version: All scripture is given by inspiration of God.

21

FOUNDATIONAL BIBLE DOCTRINES

Lesson One—INSPIRATION OF SCRIPTURE

WE NEED AN INSPIRED BIBLE.

1. God is **greater than man**.

   His **ways** are above Man's **ways** (Isaiah 55:9).

2. Man is **separated** from God by **sin** (Romans 3:23).

3. Sin has **consequences**.

   Man's **heart** has been **corrupted** (Jeremiah 17:9).

   Man's **intelligence** has been **blighted** (2 Corinthians 4:3,4).

   Man's **will** has been **affected** (John 6:44).

   Man's **conscience** has been **dulled** (Romans 1:17–25).

WHAT IS INSPIRATION?

1. Two Key Words.

   a. Theopneustos means **inspiration** (2 Timothy 3:16).

   b. Pheromai means **moved** (2 Peter 1:21).

2. Biblical Position.

   a. Verbal—God inspired the **words**.

   b. Plenary—Inspiration is **complete**.

EVIDENCE OF AN INSPIRED BIBLE.

1. Miraculous Unity.

   a. Written over **1,600** years.

   b. God used more than **40** authors.

   c. Covers ultimate issues of life, yet is without **contradiction**.

2. Accurate Prophecy.

   Prophetic passages spanning centuries have always proven to be **accurate**.

3. Archaeological Confirmation.

   Archaeological discovery has repeatedly been confirmed by **statements** of the **Bible**.

   Memory Verse: All scripture is given by inspiration of God, and is profitable for doctrine, for reproof, for correction, for instruction in righteousness (2 Timothy 3:16).

   Short Version: All scripture is given by inspiration of God.

FOUNDATIONAL BIBLE DOCTRINES

Truman Dollar, Pastor, Kansas City Baptist Temple
Kansas City, Missouri

Lesson Two—Creation

INTRODUCTION.
  I. THE DEFINITION OF CREATION.
    A. ex nehilo—Out of Nothing.
    B. By the Spoken Word.
    C. Before the Beginning.
  II. CHARACTERISTICS OF THE CREATION.
    A. Goodness in Creation.
    B. Wisdom in Creation.
  III. THE DAYS OF CREATION.
    A. The First Day—Light and Darkness.
    B. The Second Day—The Firmament.
    C. The Third Day—Seas and Land.
    D. The Fourth Day—Heavenly Lights.
    E. The Fifth Day—Fish and Fowl.
    F. The Sixth Day—Land Animals and Man.
    G. The Seventh Day—Rest.
  IV. DOCTRINES DENIED BY CREATION.
    A. Eternity of Matter.
    B. Atheism.
    C. Polytheism.
    D. Pantheism.
    E. Agnosticism.
    F. Fatalism.
CONCLUSION.

References for Study:
    Gen. 1; Ps. 19:1; 33:6,9; 104:24; 148:5; John 17:5,24; Heb. 11:3.

Memory Verse:
    In the beginning God created the heaven and the earth (Gen. 1:1).

Aim:
    To teach the method and importance of the Creation.

Point of Contact:
    When the students arrive, hand each a pencil and a sheet of paper. Give them 60 seconds to list as many types of animals as possible. Then, give them another 60 seconds to write down as many names of trees and flowers as possible. For the student

who lists the greatest number, a prize could be given. This is optional.

INTRODUCTION.

The doctrine of the Creation is one of the most fundamental. It gives us our first glimpse of the workings of God. It is also one of the most hotly contested doctrines of the Bible, because it is diametrically opposite to the accepted teachings of modern science. It does not attribute the universe and the wonders of life to chance. Instead, this doctrine pictures all things as the result of God's special creative activity. The opening chapters of Genesis are among the most complex in all Scripture. It is not our purpose to teach the complexities of Genesis one, but to clearly present the wonders of this chapter as a foundation for our belief.

I. THE DEFINITION OF CREATION.

A. ex nehilo—Out of Nothing.

There is a striking comparison between an artist's creation and that of God. An artist conceives in his mind and then brings forth into the external world. This is what happens when an artist paints a canvas, a musician composes a symphony, an engineer designs a skyscraper, or a florist makes a floral arrangement. There is first the conception in one's mind and then a bringing forth to the external world. This is exactly what God did. He conceived, created, and caused to become objective. There is also a difference between God's creation and that of these individuals. The artist had the oils and canvas. The engineer had the concrete and the steel. The florist had the flowers. However, when God created, His was quite different. Because He is infinite—He created out of nothing—ex nehilo. There was no mass, no particles of energy—nothing.

B. By the Spoken Word.

The question arises, "How did God create?" Heb. 11:3 says, "Through faith we understand that the worlds were framed by the Word of God." In this one statement we are able to see the power of God. It is beyond our finite minds. He was able to create simply by His spoken Word. There are two passages, in the Psalms that show the beauty of this spoken word. In Ps. 33:6 we read, "By the word of the Lord were the heavens made," and in verse 9, "For he spake; and it was done." The second passage is in Ps. 148:5; "Let them praise the name of the Lord: for he commanded, and they were created."

C. Before the Beginning.

Although Genesis begins, "In the beginning" that does not mean that there was not anything before that time. The Lord

26

Jesus said in His prayer to God the Father, "Thou lovedst me before the foundation of the world" (John 17:24). In other words, Jesus claims that God loved Him before the creation of everything else. And in John 17:5 Jesus asks God to glorify Him, Jesus Himself, "with the glory which I had with thee before the world was."

II. CHARACTERISTICS OF THE CREATION.

A. Goodness in Creation.

Gen. 1:4 tells us something very important about the Creation. We read, "And God saw the light, that it was good." Five other times in this chapter we find this phrase, "that it was good." When we come to Gen. 1:31, we see God sum up His entire creation; "and God saw everything that he had made, and, behold, it was very good." This remember, is not any man's judgment, but that of a holy, righteous God. God looked at all of creation and nothing was short of being good.

B. Wisdom in Creation.

In many of the Old Testament books, as the Psalms, Proverbs, and Jeremiah, the Creation is expressly declared to be the work of wisdom. Ps. 19:1 says, "The heavens declare the glory of God; and the firmament sheweth his handiwork." One can look quickly at the world around him and realize something of great wisdom was behind all of this. There is an amazing order of all these complex things. The tremendous evidence of design and order in nature encourages us to testify, with the psalmist: "O Lord, How manifold are thy works! in wisdom hast thou made them all: the earth is full of thy riches" (Ps. 104:24).

III. THE DAYS OF CREATION.

A. The First Day.

God said, "Let there be light," and immediately there was light. The light was separated from the darkness. God called the light Day; the darkness He called Night.

B. The Second Day.

The firmament was formed, the great expanse that divides the waters above it from the waters below it. He called this expanse Heaven.

C. The Third Day.

The waters under the heavenly expanse were gathered together. God called this the Seas. The dry land was called Earth.

D. The Fourth Day.

The lights in the firmament of heaven (sun, moon and stars) were made to function.

27

E. The Fifth Day.
The fish in the water and fowl in the air were created.

F. The Sixth Day.
The cattle, the creepers, and the beasts of the field were created. This is followed by the last and greatest creation of all—man, male and female.

G. The Seventh Day.
God rested from His creative activity.

IV. SIX FALSE DOCTRINES DENIED BY CREATION.
A. Eternity of Matter.
Science claims that neither energy nor matter can be destroyed or created. But the Bible teaches that there was a time when not even the universe existed. God created all.

B. Atheism.
The Atheist says there is no God, but God's Word begins by declaring His Being.

C. Polytheism.
Polytheism says that there are many gods. The Bible teaches, "In the beginning *God* created . . . ."

D. Pantheism.
This school of thought teaches that God and nature are the same. Yet, Scripture clearly presents God as the *creator* of nature.

E. Agnosticism.
This belief says it cannot be known whether there is a god or not. But the fact of creation testifies to God's existence.

F. Fatalism.
This attitude states that everything happens by fate and chance. In contrast, creation reveals that God brought the world into being and governs it by a definite plan.

CONCLUSION.
All things exist because of and through the power of God. He is the creator of all things. This fact indicates that He is a wise God and a powerful God. This wise and powerful Creator is the same God who loves men. If He is wise enough and powerful enough to create, He is surely wise and powerful enough to provide salvation, security, guidance, and help to those who trust Him. The teacher should point out that God will provide these things for those who ask, believing.

Reinforcing Illustrations:

1. For a very small investment, each student could be given a small seed with instructions on how to grow it properly. This would be extremely beneficial in showing them how with the proper amount of water and sunlight and proper temperature this plant will grow to be healthy. A timely reinforcement is that all of the essentials—water, sunlight, etc. are part of God's creation. A quick growing plant is suggested.

2. Hold two identical kinds of plants before the students. One will be wilted while the other beautiful. Ask them why the one is wilted. You will get a number of answers. You can explain that while all of them are correct, the reason is that this plant was planted on the wrong side of the house and received too much or not enough sunlight. You can then explain that God placed every plant in nature just where they would receive the proper amount of sunlight required for excellent growth. This is an excellent reinforcement on wisdom in Creation.

3. List the days of Creation. Beside them list what was created. Have your students match them up.

1. First day   A. Fish and fowl
2. Second day   B. God rested
3. Third day   C. Cattle, creepers, beasts, and man
4. Fourth day   D. Heaven
5. Fifth day   E. Day and Night
6. Sixth day   F. Seas and Earth
7. Seventh day   G. Sun, Moon, and Stars

4. List the six false doctrines that Creation denies. Beside them list what they believe. Have your students match them up.

1. Eternity of Matter   A. God and Nature
2. Atheism   B. Fate and chance
3. Polytheism   C. God cannot be proven
4. Pantheism   D. The universe has always been
5. Agnosticism   E. No god
6. Fatalism   F. Many gods

5. Creation involves God's sovereign authority. He had authority over the entire universe, even before it was created. Our society gives us many illustrations of authority. The manager of a business or factory gives directions, and his employees follow his directions. They respond to his authority. Soldiers respond to the authority of the General. Citizens obey the orders of the police. Children follow the authoritative directions of their father. The manager, the general, the policeman, the father, all have authority. They speak and things happen. God is the highest authority of all. All things are under His authority—even the universe itself. When He spoke, things happened. Creation is perhaps, the best example of God's authority. He commanded the entire world into existence.

Lesson Two: Creation
Lesson Text: Gen. 1
Craft: Creation Booklets
Materials Used:
    Paper fasteners
    Construction paper—eight colors
Instructions:

From the various colors of construction paper, cut 4"X6" rectangles, one for each child from each color. Using the appropriate color, cut the indicated patterns across the top of each rectangle and the appropriate distance from the bottom to represent sky, trees, field, lakes, etc. From the black rectangle, cut a 3½ X 1½ oval to frame the contents.

Each color, after cut, should be placed in appropriate order one on top of the other with the black frame on top and should be attached with the paper fasteners to form a small booklet. Appropriate creation verses can be written on each page.

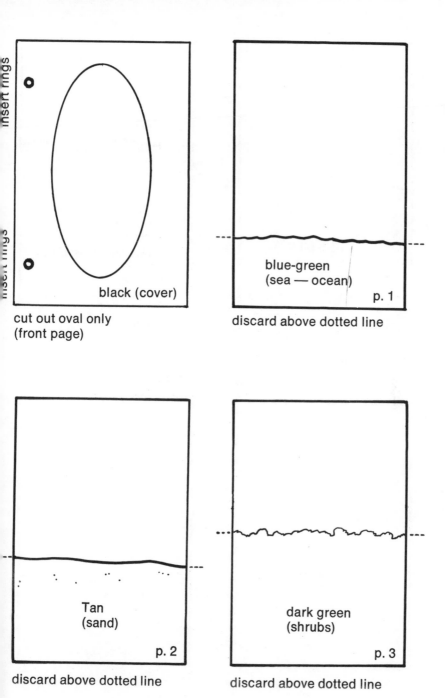

insert rings

insert rings

black (cover)

cut out oval only
(front page)

blue-green
(sea — ocean)

p. 1

discard above dotted line

Tan
(sand)

p. 2

discard above dotted line

dark green
(shrubs)

p. 3

discard above dotted line

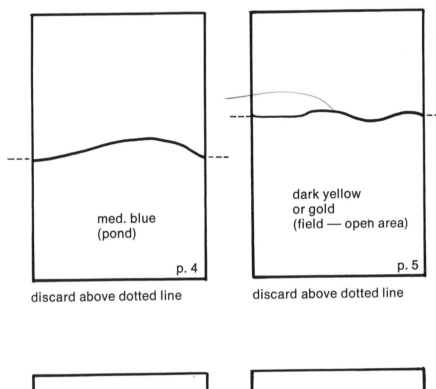

med. blue
(pond)

p. 4

discard above dotted line

dark yellow
or gold
(field — open area)

p. 5

discard above dotted line

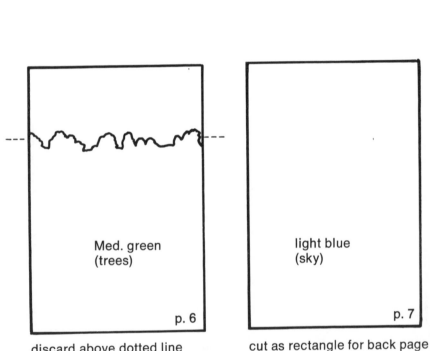

Med. green
(trees)

p. 6

discard above dotted line

light blue
(sky)

p. 7

cut as rectangle for back page

STUDY WORKSHEET

Lesson Two—CREATION

DEFINITION OF CREATION.

1. _____ creates from materials which already exist.

2. God created everything from _____.

3. God brought things into being by the _____ (Psalm 33:6,9).

4. God and Jesus existed _____ the beginning of time (John 17:5,24).

CHARACTERISTICS OF CREATION.

1. Everything God made was _____ (Genesis 1:31).

2. _____ is evident by the design and order of nature (Psalm 19:1).

DAYS OF CREATION

Day 1 _____.   Day 4 _____.

Day 2 _____.   Day 5 _____.

Day 3 _____.   Day 6 _____.

                                  Day 7 _____.

Memory Verse: In the beginning God created the heaven and the earth (Genesis 1:1).

FOUNDATIONAL BIBLE DOCTRINES

Lesson Two—CREATION

DEFINITION OF CREATION.

1. **Man** creates from materials which already exist.

2. God created everything from **nothing**.

3. God brought things into being by the **spoken word** (Psalm 33:6,9).

4. God and Jesus existed **before** the beginning of time (John 17:5,24).

CHARACTERISTICS OF CREATION.

1. Everything God made was **good** (Genesis 1:31).

2. **Wisdom** is evident by the design and order of nature (Psalm 19:1).

DAYS OF CREATION

Day 1 **light**.	Day 4 **Sun, moon, stars**.
Day 2 **heaven**.	Day 5 **fish and fowl**.
Day 3 **seas and land**.	Day 6 **man and animals**.
	Day 7 **rest**.

    Memory Verse: "In the beginning God created the heaven and the earth" (Genesis 1:1).

FOUNDATIONAL BIBLE DOCTRINES

Jack Hyles, Pastor, First Baptist Church
Hammond, Indiana

Lesson Three—God the Father

INTRODUCTION.
    I.   HE IS ETERNAL.
    II. HE IS OMNIPOTENT.
    III. HE IS OMNIPRESENT.
    IV. HE IS UNCHANGEABLE.
    V. HE IS INTIMATE.
    VI. HE IS OMNISCIENT.
  VII. HE IS HOLY.
 VIII. HE IS JUST.
    IX. HE IS LOVE.
    X. HE SHOULD BE THE OBJECT OF OUR WORSHIP.
CONCLUSION.

Reference for Study:
    Gen. 1:1,26; 17:1; Deut. 32:4; Ps. 8:1,2; 19:14; 85:10; 90:2; 99:9; 139:7–10; 147:5; Is. 6:3; 40:28; Jer. 32:17; Mal. 3:6; Matt. 3:16,17; 4:10; 28:19,20; John 4:24; 14:6,16,17; Acts 15:18; Rom. 8:15; 2 Cor. 13:14; 1 Tim. 2:5; Heb. 7:25; 1 John 4:8,16; Rev. 15:3.

Memory Verse:
    God is a Spirit: and they that worship him must worship him in spirit and in truth (John 4:24).

Aim:
    To teach my pupils the existence of God the Father and the proper attitudes they should have toward Him.

Point of Contact:
    Though we deal with the infinite things of the Bible such as the doctrine of God the Father, the Trinity, etc., we must realize that there are always things that none of us can completely understand or explain. Once a little boy was talking to his mother, and he asked her, "Mommy, what does the world set on?"
    The mother replied, "Oh, son, the world is held up by . . . er . . . ah . . . a . . . a big . . . a big man."
    A few moments passed and the boy said, "Mommy, what does the man stand on?"
    The frustrated mother said, "Er . . . a . . . son . . . a . . . er . . . a . . . the big man sits on a big rock." Hoping the boy was satisfied, she went about her activities.

A few moments later the boy said, "Mommy, what does the rock stand on?"

The confused mother said, "Son, the rock stands on . . . er . . . a . . . a . . . er . . . the rock stands on a big pole."

Hoping the boy was finished, the mother started to walk away, but the inquisitive lad said, "Mommy, what does the pole stand on?"

The frustrated and somewhat confused mother said, "Son, the pole goes all the way to the bottom. Now hush!"

Each of us will come to similar frustrations unless we have one fact established, and that is, we have a God who is our Father in Heaven and all things come from Him.

INTRODUCTION.

In order to understand God the Father, we must first understand the doctrine of the Trinity. God is a trinity. The word "trinity" comes from the word "tri" which means "three" and the word "unity" which means "oneness." This means that our God is three in one. He is not three gods, but one God. However, there are three revelations of the same God—God the Father, God the Son (Jesus), and God the Holy Spirit. In creation, God said, "Let Us make man in Our image." Notice the first person plural. In Gen. 1:1, the word for God is "Elohim," which means "plurality in one." He is one God revealed in three persons—the Father, the Son and the Holy Ghost. The Trinity was present at the baptism of Jesus (Matt. 3:16,17). The Son was in the water, the Father spoke from Heaven, and the Spirit descended in the form of a dove. The Trinity was present in the creation of man (Gen. 1:26). Note the plurality. The Trinity is mentioned in the great commission (Matt. 28:19,20). The Trinity is shown in other Bible passages such as 2 Cor. 13:14 and John 14:16,17. God the Father is the first of these persons we will discuss.

I. HE IS ETERNAL.

He is eternal. This means He always was and that He always will be. He is a Spirit who is the Creator of all things (Ps. 90:2; Is. 40:28).

II. GOD IS OMNIPOTENT.

God is omnipotent. The word "omni" means "all." The word "potent" means "powerful." In other words, God is all-powerful (Gen. 17:1; Jer. 32:17). Ah, what a blessed truth! The one whom we trust, the one who is our Creator, and the one who is our Father is all-powerful.

III. HE IS OMNIPRESENT.

He is omnipresent. This means He is everywhere (Ps. 139:

7–10). Pupils should be reminded here that this is both blessed and awesome. It is blessed in the fact that God is always with us. He never leaves us nor forsakes us, and there is no place we can go beyond His presence. It is awesome, however, when we stop to realize that He is everywhere we are, sees all we do, hears all we say, and even knows all we think.

IV. HE IS UNCHANGEABLE.

He is unchangeable. What an encouragement! Friends change; loved ones change; but our Father never changes (Mal. 3:6).

V. HE IS INTIMATE.

He is intimate. In reading Rom. 8:15, notice the word "Abba" here. It is the word "daddy" or "papa." Yes, He is the great omnipotent and omnipresent God, but He is also our papa, our daddy, and our personal God.

The eighth Psalm describes this so beautifully. In Ps. 8:1, the words, "who hast set Thy glory above the heavens," compare God to an actor or performer on a platform. His performance is on a platform on earth. The earth was not big enough for His performance, so His platform was raised to the heavens, but the heavens were not big enough for His performance. Finally the platform was raised above the heavens, for only there is there enough room for the performance of our God. Ps. 8:2 changes abruptly and mentions that He ordains strength out of the mouths of babes and sucklings. In other words, He hears the baby in the crib. This powerful God, whose performance is so mighty that the worlds cannot contain His platform, is so intimate that He is concerned about the baby crying at night. What a God! What comfort! What strength!

VI. HE IS OMNISCIENT.

He is omniscient. He knows everything (Ps. 147:5; Acts 15:18). Here is an incentive to purity of thought! This is why the psalmist said, "Let the words of my mouth, and the meditation of my heart, be acceptable in thy sight, O LORD, my strength, and my redeemer" (Ps. 19:14). No wonder he said in the same Psalm, "Cleanse thou me from secret faults." Here the psalmist is saying, "Lord, let my words be acceptable." Then, "Lord, let my thoughts be acceptable." Then, "Lord, there are some things about me I don't even know myself. Let even that be acceptable in Thy sight."

VII. HE IS HOLY.

He is holy. Notice Ps. 99:9 and Is. 6:3. It is interesting that the word "holy" is used three times in Is. 6:3. Here we have the Trinity—Holy Father, Holy Son, and Holy Spirit.

VIII.   HE IS JUST.

He is just. He is impartial in all His dealings and all His works (Deut. 32:4; Rev. 15:3).

IX.   HE IS LOVE.

He is love. Carefully study 1 John 4:8, 16. Now His holiness and justice caused Him to require penalty for our sins, but His love caused Him to send His Son to pay the price on Calvary. On the Cross God's holiness and love were shown together. Ps. 85:10 says, "Mercy and truth are met together; righteousness and peace have kissed each other." The love of God prompted Him to send His Son to die on the Cross in order that He might be just in saving us from condemnation and taking us to Heaven.

X.   HE SHOULD BE THE OBJECT OF OUR WORSHIP.

He should be the object of our worship (Matt. 4:10; John 4:24).

CONCLUSION.

The lesson should not be concluded without some discussion concerning the conditions under which God will become our Father. Notice John 14:6, especially the word, "No man cometh unto the Father, but by me." In other words, God is saying you cannot get to Him except through His Son (1 Tim. 2:5; Heb. 7:25). God is saying that if we want Him as our Father, we must have His Son as our Saviour. No one can reject the Son and have the Father. Those who say they believe in the fatherhood of God but not in the deity of Christ do not believe in the fatherhood of God either, at least not in the fatherhood of the true God. In order for one to have God as his father, he must realize he is a sinner and that sinners are condemned to an eternity without God. He must realize that God became flesh in the form of Jesus Christ, lived a perfect life, went to the Cross and paid the penalty for our sins by suffering our condemnation, and was buried and rose again after three days and three nights. He must trust that Saviour personally. At that very moment of salvation, God becomes his father and he becomes God's child.

The wise teacher would pause here and ask the pupils if they have made such a decision, and then lead them to do so.

Reinforcing Illustrations:

1. Though it is not a perfect illustration of the Trinity, the teacher could bring an egg to class. He could ask the pupils to name the different parts of the egg; that is, the shell, the white, and the yoke. He could break the egg, hold up part of the broken shell and say, "What is this?" Of course, the answer

40

would be "egg." He could hold up in a spoon part of the yoke and ask, "What is this?" The answer, of course, is "egg." He could then hold up part of the white and ask, "What is this?" The answer again is "egg." Yes, each is egg. There are three different parts to the one egg. There are three different persons to the Trinity: yet there is one God.

2. Bring some ice to class. Ask the pupils what chemical contents are found in ice. The answer is "H_2O." Then show some water. Ask them what chemical contents are in the water. The answer is "H_2O." Then discuss for a moment what happens when the water boils. Of course, it becomes vapor. What are the chemical contents of vapor? The answer once again is "H_2O." Each is H_2O. Each—ice, water, vapor—is a different manifestation of the same chemical contents. God the Father, God the Son, and God the Holy Spirit are three revelations of the same God, three in one.

3. The same could be done with an orange—the peeling, the pulp and the seed—or an apple—the peeling, the meat, and the seed. All of these are very poor illustrations and yet to the natural eye and mind they can perhaps explain in some way the great doctrine of the Trinity.

Lesson Three: God The Father
Lesson Text: John 16:23, 27
Craft: Collage of Thing God Gives Us

Materials Used:
> Old magazines with lots of pictures, at least one per student
> Blunt pointed scissors
> White glue or paste
> Multicolors of construction paper

Instructions:

A collage should be prepared to show the children when the craft is being introduced and explained. In making a collage, various pictures and words representing the theme or topic of the collage are glued on a sheet of paper. These pictures should not be placed in any particular order. They may be upside down and sideways and should overlap one another.

With the children seated at tables, distribute scissors and glue. Have magazines already on the tables. (Some pictures already cut from other magazines could be provided.) The children should have a sample to help them understand the project, but the sample should not necessarily be displayed, as this encourages copying and prevents imaginative work. Children should be encouraged to work steadily—15-30 minutes minimum required.

STUDY WORKSHEET

Lesson Three—GOD THE FATHER

1. God is eternal. He has always _____.

2. "Omni" means _____ , "potent" means _____ .

3. God _____ , _____ , _____ , everything we do.

4. Our Father never _____ (Malachi 3:6).

5. God cares about us on _____ but His glory is above the _____ (Psalm 8:1).

6. God knows more about _____ than we know about _____ .

7. The Lord our God is _____ (Psalm 99:9).

8. For God is _____ (1 John 4:8).

9. Thou Shalt _____ the Lord thy God, and him only shalt thou _____ (Matthew 4:10).

Memory Verse: God is a Spirit: and they that worship him must worship him in spirit and in truth (John 4:24).

Short Version: Worship him in spirit and in truth.

FOUNDATIONAL BIBLE DOCTRINES

Lesson Three—GOD THE FATHER

1. God is eternal. He has always **existed**.
2. "Omni" means **all**, "potent" means **powerful**.
3. God **sees**, **hears**, **knows**, everything we do.
4. Our Father never **changes** (Malachi 3:6).
5. God cares about us on **earth** but His glory is above the **heavens** (Psalm 8:1).
6. God knows more about **us** than we know about **ourselves**.
7. The Lord our God is **holy** (Psalm 99:9).
8. For God is **love** (1 John 4:8).
9. Thou Shalt **worship** the Lord thy God, and him only shalt thou **serve** (Matthew 4:10).

Memory Verse: God is a Spirit: and they that worship him must worship him in spirit and in truth (John 4:24).

Short Version: Worship him in spirit and in truth.

FOUNDATIONAL BIBLE DOCTRINES

Truman Dollar, Pastor, Kansas City Baptist Temple
Kansas City, Missouri

Lesson Four—God the Son

INTRODUCTION.
I. THE HUMANITY OF CHRIST.
   A. Jesus Called Himself a Man.
   B. Jesus Possessed Body and Soul.
   C. Jesus Had Human Characteristics.
II. THE DEITY OF CHRIST.
   A. A Vital Doctrine.
   B. Fulfills Prophecy.
   C. Taught in New Testament.
CONCLUSION.

References for Study:
   Gen. 3:15; 12:3; 15:1–7; 17:1–8,19; Is. 7:14; 9:6,7; Matt. 4:2; 8:24; 9:36; 16:16; 26:38; Mark 3:5; Luke 24:27,39; John 1:1,14,18; 3:13, 16; 4:6; 5:23,39–46; 8:23,40,56,58; 10:30; 11:35,38; 12:27,44,45; 13:13; 17:5,14,18; 19:28; 20:28–31; Acts 9:20; 1 Cor. 2:8; Gal. 3:16; Phil. 2:5; Col. 1:7; 2:9; Tit. 2:13; Jas. 2:1; 1 John 4:2,3; 5:20; Jude 25.

Memory Verse:
   And lo a voice from heaven, saying, This is my beloved Son, in whom I am well pleased (Matt. 3:17).

Aim:
   To present a clear picture of Jesus Christ as both human and divine, both man and God.

Point of Contact:
   Ask the students to list as many things as possible about Jesus—His place of birth, His miracles, His disciples, examples of His teachings, etc. This may be done either on a chalkboard, verbally, or by giving each student a pencil and paper. The creative teacher may ask the students to discuss what each thing listed shows or teaches about Jesus. These can be later related to the two major divisions of the lesson—the humanity and deity of Jesus Christ.

INTRODUCTION.
   Life's greatest question is, "What think ye of Christ, whose son is he?" Who is this great person who fills biblical literature?

What kind of nature does He possess? Since the Bible tells us that Jesus is both God and man, we will examine Him from these two aspects. When we talk about His deity, we mean that Christ is in His essential being, Holy God Himself. He is the fulness of the Godhead bodily (Col. 2:9). When we refer to His humanity, we mean that Christ through His birth in the flesh, took upon Himself the nature of man. He was not born of man, nor did He have any generic relationship to Adam. He was truly man—the Second Adam.

I. THE HUMANITY OF CHRIST.

The reality of Jesus' human nature is assumed throughout the Bible. When Gen. 3:15 promised a Redeemer, He was to come through the seed of the woman. He would be of the human family of Abraham (Gen. 12:3; 17:19), born of a virgin (Is. 7:14; 9:6,7).

A. *Jesus Called Himself a Man.*

Jesus testified to His own humanity in John 8:40: "But now ye seek to kill me, a man who hath told you the truth. . . ." He identified Himself as a man, as human.

B. *Jesus Possessed Body and Soul.*

Jesus had a physical body and a rational soul. He said of Himself, "Behold my hands and my feet, that it is I myself: handle me, and see; for a spirit hath not flesh and bones, as ye see me have" (Luke 24:39). He said His soul was "exceeding sorrowful" in Gethsemane (Matt. 26:38).

C. *Jesus Had Human Characteristics*

The Bible teaches us that He hungered (Matt. 4:2); thirsted (John 19:28); became weary (John 4:6); slept (Matt. 8:24); became troubled (John 12:27); had compassion (Matt. 9:36); became angry (Mark 3:5); groaned in spirit (John 11:38); and wept (John 11:35).

II. THE DEITY OF CHRIST.
A. *A Vital Doctrine.*

The deity of Christ is a vital doctrine. The entire purpose of the gospel is to present Jesus as God (John 20:30,31). If Jesus is not the Christ, the son of the living God, then the Gospel is an unnecessary waste. Anyone who denies that Jesus is God is antichrist (1 John 4:2,3). And, to deny the Son is to deny the Father. Christ is not the central theme of Christianity, He *is* Christianity. If He is not God, then no point of Christianity is valid.

B. Fulfills Prophecy.

The deity of Christ fulfills prophecy. Jesus, Himself, said the Old Testament spoke of Him (John 5:39–46; Luke 24:27). He is the seed of the woman, prophesied in Gen. 3:15. Abraham foresaw Him. Compare Gen. 12:1–4; 15:1–7; 17:1–8; John 8:56; Gal. 3:16. Isaiah foretold His birth (Is. 7:14; 9:6). These verses consistently show not just His coming, but His deity. The woman's seed would crush Satan. Abraham saw one who would bless all nations. Isaiah told of one who would be supernaturally born, the Mighty God, the Everlasting Father, the Prince of Peace. His deity was prophesied and fulfilled.

C. Taught in the New Testament.

The references to the deity of Christ are so numerous and explicit that no intelligent or honest person who reads the New Testament with an open mind could possibly overlook the fact that Jesus Christ is declared to be very God. The New Testament ascribes divine names to Christ. His human name, Jesus, means Saviour. In John 1:1,14, He is called the Word who was with God and was God. He possessed all the fulness of the Godhead (Col. 2:9). He is called the "only begotten" (John 1:18; 3:16), the "firstborn" (Col. 1:15), the "Son of the living God" (Matt. 16:16), "My Lord and my God" (John 20:28), "great God and our Saviour" (Tit. 2:13), the "true God" (1 John 5:20), and "Lord of glory" (1 Cor. 2:8). The term Christ, itself, is not a name but a title. It corresponds to the Hebrew "Messiah" and means "Jehovah's anointed."

As God, Jesus existed before His birth at Bethlehem. He was sent into the world (John 17:18). He *became* flesh (John 1:14). He was from above (John 8:23). He was not of the world (John 17:14). He descended out of Heaven (John 3:13). He enjoyed glory with the Father before the world was created (John 17:5). He was before all things and created all things (Col. 1:17).

Jesus claimed to be God. He said that He and the Father were one (John 10:30), and repeatedly stated that He was sent from the Father (John 5:23; 12:44,45). He said that He was the great "I am" (John 8:58). Even the Jews recognized this to be a claim of deity and sought to kill him for blasphemy. There can be no doubt that Jesus claimed to be God.

His apostles and disciples regarded Him as God. Read the testimony of Peter (Matt. 16:16), Paul (Acts 9:20; Col. 2:9; Phil. 2:5), James (Jas. 2:1), Thomas (John 20:28), and Jude (Jude 25). Jesus unquestionably received worship from His followers. No one but God is due worship. Therefore, Jesus is either God or allowed a false act. If the latter were true, He would not even be a good or honest man. Jesus was either a liar, a lunatic, or the Lord of the universe. He claimed to be Lord (John 13:13), and His life and character proved him to be.

CONCLUSION.

One cannot understand the life, ministry, and substitutionary death of Christ apart from His deity. If He were not God, why was He born of a virgin? Why did He claim to be of preexistent, divine origin? How could He die for the sins of men if He were only a man? How could a mere man rise from the dead? You see, there is much more at stake than just one area of doctrine. If Jesus were not God, then He could not be our Saviour.

The ultimate proof of the deity of Christ is the changed lives of those who have received Him as their Saviour. He promised eternal life to all who would believe in Him. That life is available to you right now.

The teacher should testify of his faith in Christ and give the students opportunity to receive Him.

Reinforcing Illustrations:

1. Ask members of the class to name the things which are most valuable to them. Children may name a favorite toy, game, or even a favorite dessert. Older children and teens might list items of clothing, records, or a car. Even adults may participate in this type of exercise. After several examples have been given, ask the class members if they would be able to give away that favorite item to a total stranger and ask nothing in return. Point out that this is exactly what God did in giving His Son Jesus Christ to die on the Cross. He took that which He treasured most and gave it to totally undeserving sinners, asking nothing from them in return. This illustration is especially powerful and dramatic when used with Young Married Adults who have small children. Ask them if they would be willing to give up those children for the sake of undeserving sinners.

2. Bring several items to class that can be easily identified by the students. Show them to the class one item at a time. Ask them to look at the item, feel the item, and use the item. Then, ask them to identify the item based upon how it looks, feels, and is used. If it looks and feels like a book and can be read like a book, then it must be a book. If it looks and feels like a pencil and can be used to write, it must be a pencil. Impress on the students that things can be identified by the way they look, feel, and act. As man, Jesus looked, felt, and acted as a man—yet without sin. As God, Jesus showed divine wisdom and performed divine acts. As we look at Jesus through the Scriptures, we can clearly see that He was very much man and very much God. He was the God-Man.

3. Illustrate the importance of a specific purpose by using ordinary things in an absurd way. For children, bring a shoe and try wearing it as a hat. Try writing a message with the eraser end of a pencil. Use your imagination. The more obviously absurd

the illustration, the more effective with the children. For teens and adults, merely mentioning the absurd is effective. For example, a dentist does not perform brain surgery. An auto mechanic does not pull teeth. If we need to borrow money, we go to a bank, not a dry cleaners. Everything in life has a specific use or purpose. So it is with Christ. He came to seek and to save the lost (Luke 19:10). Everything else that Jesus did was incidental to this central theme. His specific purpose in living, dying, and rising from the dead was the salvation of souls. To suggest otherwise is as absurd as wearing a shoe for a hat.

4. Since one of the main points of this lesson is the Deity of Christ, it may be useful to repeat one of the illustrations under God the Father, showing Christ's position as a part of the Holy Trinity.

Lesson Four: God The Son
Lesson Text: John 1:14
Craft: Manger and Child

Materials Needed:
Medium weight cardboard
Light weight cardboard
Easter basket grass in green, yellow, or white
Flat wooden spoons as used for ice cream cups
Pipe cleaners—white or yellow (1 per child—6″ long)
2½ X 4″ strips of material
Pens

Instructions:

Cut 2½ X 4″ rectangles from the cardboard. Fold these in half and cut 2 ⅛″ slits into the fold ¼″ from the end. From the cardboard cut 2 "X's" per child. These should have 1″ arms. The 2 "X's" should be fitted into the slits of the folded paper and this opened to form a trough. Grass should be placed into this trough.

A child form should be made with the spoons. A pipe cleaner wrapped around its middle and each end formed into ovals to represent hands. This should be wrapped in the material and placed into the cradle.

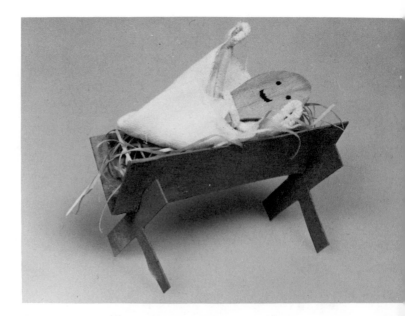

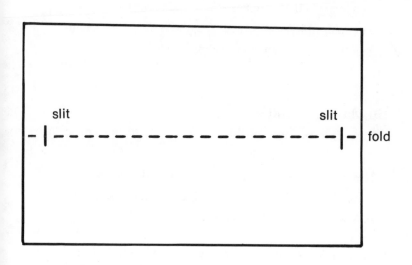

slit   slit

fold

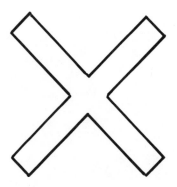

STUDY WORKSHEET

Lesson Four—GOD THE SON

THE HUMANITY OF CHRIST.

1. Jesus identified Himself as a _____ and as _____ .

2. Jesus had a physical _____ and a _____ soul.

3. Jesus had human characteristics, needs of:

    1.   3.

    2.   4.

THE DEITY OF CHRIST.

1. The entire purpose of the _____ is to present Jesus as _____ (John 20:30,31).

2. Christ's deity was _____ in the Old Testament.

3. Jesus claimed to be _____ . He said that He and the Father were _____ (John 10:30).

Memory Verse: And lo a voice from heaven saying, This is my beloved Son, in whom I am well pleased (Matthew 3:17).

Short Version: This is my beloved Son.

FOUNDATIONAL BIBLE DOCTRINES

Lesson Four—GOD THE SON

THE HUMANITY OF CHRIST.

1. Jesus identified Himself as a **man** and as **human**.

2. Jesus had a physical **body** and a **rational** soul.

3. Jesus had human characteristics, needs of:

   1. **hunger**   3. **weariness**

   2. **thirst**   4. **anxiety**

THE DEITY OF CHRIST.

1. The entire purpose of the **gospel** is to present Jesus as **God** (John 20:30,31).

2. Christ's deity was **prophesied** in the Old Testament.

3. Jesus claimed to be **God**. He said that He and the Father were **one** (John 10:30).

Memory Verse: And lo a voice from heaven saying, This is my beloved Son, in whom I am well pleased (Matthew 3:17).

Short Version: This is my beloved Son.

FOUNDATIONAL BIBLE DOCTRINES

Truman Dollar, Pastor, Kansas City Baptist Temple
Kansas City, Missouri

Lesson Five—God the Holy Spirit

INTRODUCTION.
I. THE HOLY SPIRIT IS A PERSON.
   A. He is Given a Name.
   B. He has Attributes of Personality.
   C. He has Appeared on Earth.
   D. He is Rational.
   E. He has Personal Characteristics.
II. THE HOLY SPIRIT IS GOD.
   A. He is Called God.
   B. He has Divine Attributes.
   C. He Performs Divine Acts.
III. THE HOLY SPIRIT IS ACTIVE.
   A. He Glorifies Christ.
   B. He Convicts.
   C. He Regenerates.
   D. He Commissions.
   E. He Empowers.
   F. He Produces Fruit.
IV. THE HOLY SPIRIT IS MISUNDERSTOOD.
   A. As Impersonal.
   B. As Removing Responsibility.
   C. As Concealing the Gospel.
   D. As Exclusive.
CONCLUSION.

References for Study:
   Gen. 1:2; 2:7; Job 33:4; Ps. 139:7; Matt. 3:16; 10:19,20; 12:28;
John 6:63; 14:17,26; 15:26; 16:8,13,14; Acts 1:8; 5:3,4; 7:51; 13:2;
Rom. 8:26,27; 15:13; 1 Cor. 2:7–14; 3:16; 6:19; 12:7–11; Gal.
5:22,23; Eph. 1:13; 4:30; Phil. 2:5–8; Heb. 9:14; 2 Pet. 1:21.

Memory Verse:
   But the Comforter, which is the Holy Ghost, whom the Father
will send in my name, he shall teach you all things, and bring all
things to your remembrance, whatsoever I have said unto you
(John 14:26).

Aim:
   To give each student a proper understanding of the Holy
Spirit as a person of the Godhead.

Point of Contact:
Ask the students to describe things that the wind does, for example, whistling through tree limbs, rustling dry leaves, or piling up snow drifts. Then ask the students to describe the wind itself. No one can see the wind, only the things it does. Likewise, Christians do not see the Holy Spirit but can learn much about Him from what He does in Scripture.

INTRODUCTION.
Like a giant pendulum, the doctrine of the Holy Spirit is swung from one extreme to the other. For years, people tried to sidestep this great doctrine lest they be labeled Pentecostals. Then, with the coming of the Charismatic movement, hundreds have suddenly joined the group declaring the gift of tongues to be the evidence of the Holy Spirit. Men have created much confusion and error concerning the personality, operation, and gifts of the Holy Spirit. People of good character and deep conviction are misguided and hold wrong views on this most important doctrine.

It is impossible to live a victorious Christian life unless we are aware of the person and work of the Holy Spirit. We should know Him as a divine person of the Godhead trinity and not as an impersonal force. This divine person was active in creation and is evidenced throughout the Old Testament. In the New Testament period, He convicts of sin, is active in the new birth, seals, endues, teaches, and guides the Christian. It is important to sort out fact from fancy in this crucial doctrine.

I. THE HOLY SPIRIT IS A PERSON.
The Scripture teaches that the Holy Spirit is not just a force or an impersonal power. He is a genuine person. Several things indicate this.

A. He is Given a Name.
Jesus called the Holy Spirit the Comforter (John 14:26). He also referred to Him as the Spirit of Truth (John 14:17).

B. He has Attributes of Personality.
He is described as one who will guide us into all truth. The guiding aspect is that of a person (John 16:13). The Scripture also tells us that He will bring to our remembrance certain things (John 14:26). John 15:26 tells us that He testifies of Jesus Christ. This is a designation of a personal activity. John 16:14 tells us that He glorifies Jesus Christ. In 1 Cor. 12:11 we are told that He distributes divine gifts. In Eph. 1:13 and 4:30 we are told that He seals unto the day of redemption. We are told in Rom. 8:26,27 that He heals our infirmities and that He intercedes for us in prayer. These are all attributes of personality.

C. He has Appeared on Earth.

He distinguished Himself as an individual person of the Godhead at the baptism of the Lord Jesus when He appeared in a visible form that in the manner of a dove descended from above (Matt. 3:16).

D. He is Rational.

In 1 Cor. 12:7–11, Paul tells us that Christian gifts are from the Spirit. The Spirit distributes these gifts severally as He will. "As He will" indicates that the Holy Spirit acts at His own choice and judgment. 1 Cor. 2:7–10 tells us that the wisdom of God is made known to us by the Spirit of God who searches all things. He intelligently looks beyond all that the eye can see, to those regions where God's plan for man developed. He reveals these things unto men.

E. He has Personal Characteristics.

He can exercise power (Rom. 15:13). The Holy Spirit is treated as a person. He is grieved (Eph. 4:30). He is resisted (Acts 7:51). He may be lied to (Acts 5:3,4).

II. THE HOLY SPIRIT IS GOD.

A. He is Called God.

When Peter rebuked Ananias, saying he had lied to the Holy Spirit, he repeated the charge, saying that Ananias and Sapphira had agreed to lie to God (Acts 5:3,4). In 1 Cor. 3:16, Christians are called the temple of God. Later, we are called the temple of the Holy Spirit (1 Cor. 6:19). Both of these cases indicate that God and the Holy Spirit are one.

B. He has Divine Attributes.

He is called eternal in Heb. 9:14. That He is all-wise, or omniscient, is indicated in 1 Cor. 2:10, for we are told that He searches all things. According to Ps. 139:7, the Holy Spirit is able to be present everywhere at once, or omnipresent. The Holy Spirit is all-powerful—omnipotent. Christ was put to death in the flesh, but was quickened, or brought to life, by the spirit (1 Pet. 3:18). Power to overcome death is a divine capacity.

C. He Performs Divine Acts.

The Holy Spirit was active in creation of both matter and life (Gen. 1:2; 2:7; Job 33:4). Only a divine individual is capable of creation. Jesus cast out devils by the Spirit of God (Matt. 12:28). Divine gifts were given by the Spirit (1 Cor. 12:7,10). Writers of Scripture were moved to write by the Spirit (2 Pet. 1:21). The Spirit gives life to the souls who believe in Jesus Christ (John 6:63).

III. THE HOLY SPIRIT IS ACTIVE.

A. *He Glorifies Christ.*

Jesus promised to send a Comforter following His ascension into Heaven. According to John 16:14, one of the major activities of this Comforter—the Holy Spirit—is to bring glory to Jesus Christ.

B. *He Convicts.*

John 16:8 says that the Spirit reproves—that is, convicts or convinces—the world of sin, righteousness, and judgment.

C. *He Regenerates.*

As we have already seen, it is the Spirit who quickens, or gives life (John 6:63). In Tit. 3:5–7 He is described as washing or renewing us.

D. *He Commissions.*

It was the Spirit of God who designated Paul and Barnabas for a missionary ministry (Acts 13:2).

E. *He Empowers.*

The Holy Spirit gives Christians special power in several areas: the power to witness (Acts 1:8); to understand spiritual things (1 Cor. 2:7–14; 12:3,4); to remember (John 14:26); and to preach (Matt. 10:19,20).

F. *He Produces Fruit.*

Gal. 5:22,23 list the fruit—or qualities—the Holy Spirit will produce in the lives of believers. Notice that He produces this fruit because He dwells within the believer. The Spirit does not indwell the believer because the believer produces fruit.

IV. THE HOLY SPIRIT IS MISUNDERSTOOD.

A. *As Impersonal.*

The Holy Spirit is regarded by some as a de-personalized force. Some people think the Holy Spirit is not a person, but rather a nonpersonal entity. They need to consider the elements we have pointed out above.

B. *As Removing Responsibility.*

Some think the Holy Spirit is to provide them a happiness without responsibility. They are seeking only to gain special joys, special hallelujahs, without recognizing that the Spirit came not to give us a shout, but to give us power to perform certain duties.

C. As Concealing the Gospel.

There is the error that the Spirit comes to conceal communication. They believe that they are given the ability to speak in languages that conceal the gospel to the unsaved. The opposite is true. The Spirit came that they might be witnesses to the lost and a sign to the unbeliever, not to the believer.

D. As Exclusive.

There is an error of the exclusive-elite—the proud attitude that "we have the whole gospel." In contrast, those who have the Spirit are meek, gentle, and humble. Phil. 2:5–8 describes those who have the mind of Christ as making themselves of no report and making the Lord all-and-all.

CONCLUSION.

The Holy Spirit is a person. He is part of the Holy Trinity. He is the activating force in the life of all Christians. Without His ministry Christians are powerless and fruitless.

The teacher should emphasize that even though the Holy Spirit is as invisible as the wind, He is still a very real and very active person who is always ready to guide and assist Christians in their daily living.

Reinforcing Illustrations:

1. Inflate a clear plastic bag. Pass it among the students, allowing them to feel the bag by lightly squeezing it. Hold the bag up before the class and ask them to describe what they *see* inside. The bag obviously contains something. The students could feel that for themselves. Yet, no one is able to see what the bag contains. So it is with the Holy Spirit. His presence can be felt and known through Scripture. Yet, He cannot be seen. A variation of this illustration involves an inflated balloon tied closed with a string or rubber band. When the string is released, ask the students to describe what they *see* coming out of the balloon.

2. This illustration is limited only by the teacher's imagination and the time allotted for reinforcing the lesson. The more elaborate its presentation, the more effective it will be with children. It can also be very effective with adults. The point is, many things on which we depend are useless without a power source. Lights, electric appliances—both large and small, cars, many toys, and countless other items cannot be used without a power source. A creative teacher will bring several such items to class. Students will easily remember the spectacle of a teacher helplessly trying to use an array of small appliances or toys that either have not been plugged into a wall socket or do not have proper batteries. Christians are just as useless unless they are

plugged into the divine power source, God's great trans-
former—the Holy Spirit.

3. Since one of the main points of this lesson is the Deity of
the Holy Spirit, it may be useful to repeat one of the illustrations
under God the Father, showing the Holy Spirit's position as a
part of the Holy Trinity.

Lesson Five: God The Holy Spirit
Lesson Text: 1 Cor. 6:19a
Craft: The Heart
Materials Needed:
   Red, yellow, white construction paper
   Black ink or crayon
   Glue

Instructions:
   In advance, cut shapes to represent the bust of a boy or girl from yellow construction paper. Also cut heart shapes from the red construction paper, with a door in the center of each heart. And, cut dove shapes from the white construction paper.

Hand out to the children each of the above shapes. They may draw a face on the bust of the boy or girl with the black ink or crayon. Then, let them glue the heart onto the bust, leaving the area of the door unglued. Let them fold back the door and paste the dove in the heart. They may then write the memory verse on the bottom of the bust.

cut on fold and glue
one side to page
to make door

red

white

STUDY WORKSHEET

Lesson Five—GOD THE HOLY SPIRIT

THE HOLY SPIRIT IS A PERSON.

1. The Holy Spirit was called:

    _____ (John 14:26).

    _____ (John 14:17).

2. The Holy Spirit has personality attributes of:

    _____   _____   _____

    _____   _____

3. The Holy Spirit has personality characteristics of _____ ,

    _____ , _____ .

THE HOLY SPIRIT IS GOD.

1. Ananias and Sapphira not only lied to the _____ , but also to _____ (Acts 5:3,4).

2. The Holy Spirit's divine attributes are: _____ , _____ , _____ , _____ , and others.

3. Writers of the Scriptures were moved by _____ inspiration of the Holy Spirit.

THE HOLY SPIRIT IS ACTIVE.

1. He _____ Christ (John 16:14).

2. He _____ the world of sin (John 16:8).

3. He _____ , or gives new life (John 6:63).

4. He produces _____ because He dwells in the _____ (Galatians 5:22,23).

Memory Verse: But the Comforter, which is the Holy Ghost, whom the Father will send in my name, he shall teach you all things, and bring all things to your remembrance, whatsoever I have said unto you (John 14:26).

Short Version: The Holy Ghost . . . shall teach you all things.

FOUNDATIONAL BIBLE DOCTRINES

Lesson Five—GOD THE HOLY SPIRIT

THE HOLY SPIRIT IS A PERSON

1. The Holy Spirit was called:

   Comforter (John 14:26).

   Truth (John 14:17).

2. The Holy Spirit has personality attributes of:

   guidance   **testifies of Christ**   **distributes gifts**

   remembrance   **glorifies Christ**

3. The Holy Spirit has personality characteristics of **power, grief, rejection**.

THE HOLY SPIRIT IS GOD.

1. Ananias and Sapphira not only lied to the **Holy Spirit**, but also to **God** (Acts 5:3,4).

2. The Holy Spirit's divine attributes are: **eternal**, **all-wise**, **omnipresent**, **omnipotent**, and others.

3. Writers of the Scriptures were moved by **divine** inspiration of the Holy Spirit.

THE HOLY SPIRIT IS ACTIVE.

1. He **glorifies** Christ (John 16:14).

2. He **convicts** the world of sin (John 16:18).

3. He **regenerates**, or gives new life (John 6:63).

4. He produces **fruit** because He dwells in the **believer** (Galatians 5:22,23).

Memory Verse: But the Comforter, which is the Holy Ghost, whom the Father will send in my name, he shall teach you all things, and bring all things to your remembrance, whatsoever I have said unto you (John 14:26).

Short Version: The Holy Ghost . . . shall teach you all things.

FOUNDATIONAL BIBLE DOCTRINES

Jerry Falwell, Pastor, Thomas Road Baptist Church
Lynchburg, Virginia

Lesson Six—Salvation

INTRODUCTION.
I.   ITS DEFINITION.
    A. The Meaning.
    B. The Usage.
II. ITS NECESSITY.
    A. Man's Sin.
    B. God's Righteousness.
III. ITS PROVISION.
    A. Through Christ.
    B. To God's Satisfaction.
IV. ITS CONDITION.
    A. Repentance.
    B. Belief.
    C. Acceptance.
V.   ITS ASSURANCE.
VI. ITS SCOPE.
    A. Past.
    B. Present.
    C. Future.
CONCLUSION.

References for Study:
Gen. 6:5; Ex. 34:6,7; Is. 53:5,6; Jer. 17:9; Matt. 1:21; 9:12,13; Mark 7:20–23; 9:43–48; 10:45; Luke 13:3; 16:22–31; 19:10; John 1:12; 3:16,17; 5:24; 8:21,24; 10:11, 15–18,27–30; Acts 4:10–12; 5:31; 13:38; 17:31; 20:21; Rom. 1:21–32; 3:19–23; 4:5; 5:1,12,18,19; 6:1–16; 8:1,5–9; 10:9,10; 12:1,2; 1 Cor. 6:11,19; 15:1–4; 2 Cor. 4:3,4; 5:21; Eph. 2:1–3,8; 1 Thes. 4:13–18; 1 Tim. 1:15; 2 Tim. 2:15; Tit. 2:11–15; Heb. 4:14–16; 9:28; 1 Pet. 2:24; 2 Pet. 1:3,4; 1 John 1:8,9; 2:12; 5:9,10,13; Jude 11–13; Rev. 20:11–15.

Memory Verse:
He that believeth on the Son hath everlasting life: and he that believeth not the Son shall not see life; but the wrath of God abideth on him (John 3:36).

Aim:
To provide the student with a better understanding of salvation, so that they might accept Christ if lost, or better appreciate Him if already saved.

Point of Contact:
The teacher should bring a gift-wrapped box to class and display it before the students. He may encourage the students to try guessing the contents of the box. The teacher should also put a gospel tract, or a paper with the word "Salvation" written on it, inside the box. When the box is opened, he can use this tract or paper to illustrate that Salvation is a gift from God.

INTRODUCTION.
Salvation is a big word. It is big in the sense that it covers the meaning of many other words. To be saved means to be delivered, to be forgiven, to be pardoned, to be redeemed, to be restored, and much more. The word suggests that there are those who need to be saved. The Bible leaves no doubt who those people are. In 1 Tim. 1:15 we read, "This is a faithful saying, and worthy of all acceptation, that Christ Jesus came into the world to save sinners . . . ." Jesus came into the world to save, that is, to provide salvation for, sinful men.

I. ITS DEFINITION.
    A. The Meaning.
The word Salvation simply means deliverance. It is commonly used to describe the act by which a person is delivered from a danger that threatens him. We speak of a person being saved from drowning, or from a burning building, or from a sinking ship. In each case, three things are taken for granted: 1.) that the person to be saved was in danger; 2.) that someone saw his peril and went to his rescue; and 3.) that the rescuer was successful in his mission, delivered the person from his perilous plight, and thus saved him.

    B. The Usage.
The words save, saved, Saviour, and Salvation occur many times in the Bible and have exactly the same meaning in the spiritual sense. The name Jesus centers in the idea of salvation. Jesus is the Greek form of the Hebrew name Joshua. Joshua means Jehovah saves. What a great name for the commander-in-chief of Israel's army to bear! It reminded him and his soldiers when they went into battle that Salvation is of the Lord. It was because of the meaning of this name that it was given to our Lord at His birth. "Thou shalt call his name JESUS: for he shall save his people from their sins" (Matt. 1:21). Unless we know our Lord Jesus Christ as Saviour, we do not really know Him, for His name reveals what He is. It is equally clear from this passage that Jesus did not come to save people from social injustice or governmental oppression. He came to save people from their sins. Man needs to be saved, because he is a sinner. Describing His own work, our Lord said, "The Son of man is

come to seek and to save that which was lost" (Luke 19:10). Those who are not saved are lost. This is the Bible usage of the word Salvation—saving lost sinners.

II. ITS NECESSITY.

A. Man's Sin.

Man's sinful nature is a fact. In time, this nature makes itself evident through sinful thoughts, words, deeds, and an attitude of enmity to God. The Bible makes this clear in the following passages of Scripture: Rom. 5:12,18,19; 6:16; 8:5–8; Gen. 6:5; Eph. 2:1–3; 2 Cor. 4:3,4; Is. 53:6; Jer. 17:9; Mark 7:20–23; Rom. 1:21–32; 3:19–23. It will be evident to all from these passages that man is: 1.) a sinner, needing forgiveness; 2.) lost, needing to be found; 3.) doomed, needing deliverance; 4.) guilty, needing pardon; 5.) spiritually dead, needing life; 6.) blind, needing illumination; and 7.) a slave, needing liberation. Man is utterly helpless to save himself.

B. God's Righteousness.

God is holy and must punish sin. He will "by no means clear the guilty" (Ex. 34:6,7). He has revealed His hatred of sin and His sentence against all who die in their sins—eternal banishment from His presence. Read John 8:21–24; Mark 9:43–48; Luke 16:22–31; Jude 11–13; Rev. 20:11–15. The conclusion is obvious. Since man is a sinner and God is righteous, the sinner needs to be delivered—or saved—from the penalty of his sins.

III. ITS PROVISION.

A. Through Christ.

The gospel is the good news that God, in wondrous grace, has abundantly provided this Salvation through the person and work of His beloved Son. According to Matt. 1:21, He came to be the Saviour of sinners. The Son of God, equal and eternal with the Father and the Holy Spirit, became the incarnate in order to provide Salvation. See John 3:16,17; 10:11,15–18; Mark 10:45; Matt. 9:12,13.

B. To God's Satisfaction.

Through Christ's death and resurrection, this Salvation has been provided to God's complete satisfaction. As Christ willingly hung on the Cross, He assumed the full liability of our guilt and sin, bore our sins in His own body, and died as a substitutionary sacrifice on behalf of sinners. All God's judgment against sin fell on Him, and all God's righteous claims against the sinners were fully satisfied, on our behalf, by Christ's death. God indicated His complete acceptance of this sacrifice of Christ by raising Him from the dead and seating Him at His own right hand. Read 1 Cor. 15:1–4; 2 Cor. 5:21; 1 Pet. 2:24; Is. 53:5; Rom. 5:6–9; Acts 4:10–12; 5:31; 17:31.

IV. ITS CONDITION.

Since Christ has accomplished, by sacrifice of Himself, all the work needed for the sinner's Salvation, what must the sinner do in order to experience this Salvation?

A. Repentance.

He must repent. Repentance is simply a change of mind which results in a change of attitude toward sin, self, the Saviour, and Salvation. This change of mind is, in turn, evidenced by a change of action (Luke 13:3; Acts 17:31; 20:21). The sinner's indifference will be replaced by an earnest desire for Salvation. He will confess his helpless, hopeless, and hell-deserving condition.

B. Belief.

He must believe the gospel, or the testimony of God concerning the person and work of Christ (1 John 5:9,10). As a lost and guilty sinner, he must believe that Christ died for him, individually; that Christ bore his sins, took his place, and by His death accomplished all the work needed for his Salvation (Rom. 4:5).

C. Acceptance.

He must accept the Lord Jesus Christ, by a definite act of his will, as his own personal Saviour, with the commitment to henceforth acknowledge Him as the supreme Lord of his life (John 1:12; Rom. 10:9,10).

V. ITS ASSURANCE.

How may one know for certain that he is saved? By the Word of God. God declares plainly and in black and white that every soul trusting in His Son is forgiven, saved, the possessor of eternal life, and secure forever. Read Acts 13:38; 1 John 2:12; Eph. 2:8; 1 Cor. 6:11, 1 John 5:13; Rom. 5:1; 8:1; John 10:27–30.

VI. ITS SCOPE.

A. Past.

The past involves Salvation from sin's penalty or consequences. Since Christ has endured the full penalty which was due to our sins, the believer is delivered from its dread consequences (John 5:24; Rom. 8:1).

B. Present.

The present involves Salvation from sin's power or control. Because of the Holy Spirit's indwelling presence, plus the impartation of a divine nature, the believer is now delivered from the dominion of sin in his life (1 Cor. 6:19; 2 Pet. 1:3,4; Rom. 6:1–14). This does not mean that the believer is incapable of sin.

Far from it! For he still possesses the evil nature, the flesh. It does mean that to the extent to which he avails himself of the means God has provided, he will be free from sin as the dominating factor in his life. This present deliverance will depend on: 1.) the reading and study of and obedience to the Word of God (2 Tim. 2:15); 2.) the keeping constantly in touch with God by prayer (Heb. 4:14–16); 3.) the yielding of one's body to God for both a righteous and useful life (Rom. 6:13; 12:1,2); and 4.) the prompt confession to God and the forsaking of all known sin (1 John 1:8,9; Tit. 2:11–15).

C. Future.

The future involves Salvation from sin's presence. This will take place at the coming of Christ, when He will raise the dead and change the living so that they will have bodies incapable of sin, decay, and death. This is the final aspect of Salvation (Heb. 9:28; 1 Thes. 4:13–18).

CONCLUSION.

The teacher should not lose this opportunity to lead members of his class to Jesus Christ. He should offer a brief testimony of his own Salvation, and challenge the students to accept Christ as personal Saviour.

Reinforcing Illustrations.

1. Ask the members of the class to list dangerous situations. Discuss with them why each situation is perilous. Determine what is at stake—money, reputation, property, health, life. Discuss what steps could be taken to avoid each dangerous situation. The most dangerous situation anyone can face is going through life unprepared for eternity. When used at the close of the lesson, this illustration can provide an effective opportunity for evangelism.

2. This illustration is a reverse application of one discussed under God the Son. Ask the students to list things they would like to have, places they would like to go, or people they would like to meet. Then ask what they would be willing to give up to have their wish come true. God wants to save sinners so much that He was willing to give up His only Son. It was the only way to provide a just Salvation, and God was willing to pay the price.

3. Things receive value in accordance with what people are willing to pay for them. This is the law of supply and demand. When oil became less available the price climbed rapidly. Diamonds are so valuable because they are rare. Even gold, if it were as plentiful as lead, would be of no great value. Adults and teens can easily understand this concept. A thirsty man will pay dearly for water. A dying man will give his fortune for life.

Things are only valuable if people are willing to pay for them. Man, of himself, has no value. He is sinful. He is incapable of good. He is spiritually dead. Yet God, in love, saw fit to place a value on man. God was willing to pay the ultimate price, to put the ultimate value on man. Man, worthless in his own right, can become a priceless possession by accepting God's ultimate gift, Salvation.

4. Ask the class to describe the perfect gift. Add to their suggestions: extreme value, never able to be worn out or lost, needed, brings joy and satisfaction, never out of style, never loses its attraction, etc. That gift, of course, is Salvation, provided freely by God to all who believe on His Son Jesus Christ.

Lesson Six: Salvation
Lesson Text: John 3:16
Craft: Salvation Chain

Materials Needed:

Black, red, white, green, and gold construction paper cut in strips 6" long and 1" wide

Glue

Instructions:

Make a sample chain for the children to copy.

Explain the color representations to the children before they begin their craft:

Black—Sin   Green—growth in Christ

Red—blood of Christ   Gold—Heaven

White—cleansing/forgiveness

Each child should be given the five various paper strips and should make a chain. The meaning of the various colors (in appropriate order) should be reviewed.

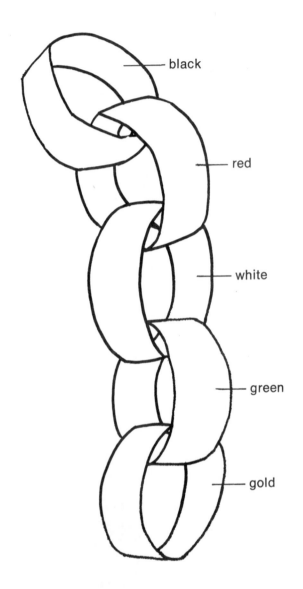

black

red

white

green

gold

STUDY WORKSHEET

Lesson Six—SALVATION

Definition: Salvation means _____.

THE NECESSITY OF SALVATION.

1. Man's _____ nature is a fact (Romans 3:10).

2. God is _____ and must punish _____.

ITS PROVISION.

1. _____ came to be the _____ of sinners (Matthew 1:21).

2. Christ's _____ and _____ completed God's _____.

ITS CONDITION.

1. Repentance is a change of _____, _____, and _____.

2. One must _____ the gospel.

3. One must _____ the Lord Jesus Christ.

Memory Verse: He that believeth on the Son hath everlasting life: and he that believeth not the Son shall not see life; but the wrath of God abideth on him (John 3:36).

Short Version: He that believeth on the Son hath everlasting life.

FOUNDATIONAL BIBLE DOCTRINES

Lesson Six—SALVATION

Definition: Salvation means **deliverance**.

THE NECESSITY OF SALVATION.

1. Man's **sin** nature is a fact (Romans 3:10).

2. God is **righteous** and must punish **sin**.

ITS PROVISION.

1. **Christ** came to be the **Saviour** of sinners (Matthew 1:21).

2. Christ's **death** and **resurrection** completed God's **plan**.

ITS CONDITION.

1. Repentance is a change of **mind**, **attitude**, and **action**.

2. One must **believe** the gospel.

3. One must **accept** the Lord Jesus Christ.

   Memory Verse: He that believeth on the Son hath everlasting life: and he that believeth not the Son shall not see life; but the wrath of God abideth on him (John 3:36).

   Short Version: He that believeth on the Son hath everlasting life.

FOUNDATIONAL BIBLE DOCTRINES

A. V. Henderson, Pastor, Temple Baptist Church
Detroit, Michigan

Lesson Seven—Baptism

INTRODUCTION.
  I. A PROPER UNDERSTANDING.
     A. The Proper Authority.
     B. The Proper Candidate.
     C. The Proper Purpose.
     D. The Proper Mode.
 II. SOME IMPROPER CANDIDATES.
     A. Those with Impure Hearts.
     B. Those with Incomplete Message.
     C. Those with Insincere Belief.
III. PROPER FOR OBEDIENCE.
     A. A Multitude.
     B. A Eunuch.
     C. A Jailor.
CONCLUSION.

References for Study:
  Matt. 28:18–20; Acts 2:41; 8:5–24, 26–39; 16:33; Rom. 6:4; Eph. 2:8.

Memory Verse:
  Therefore we are buried with him by baptism into death: that like as Christ was raised up from the dead by the glory of the Father, even so we also should walk in newness of life (Rom. 6:4).

Aim:
  To teach what the Bible says about Baptism and why it is important.

Point of Contact:
  Ask members of the class to describe the Baptism of Jesus. Have them give all the information possible about this important event in the life of Christ. Then, ask the class what John the Baptist demanded of those who came to him for Baptism.

INTRODUCTION.
  There is much confusion and misinformation on the doctrine of Baptism. It will be necessary to combat many preconceived

ideas. Because of the false teaching that has been done for centuries on this subject, it will be necessary to lay a new foundation in the minds of the students. It will not be possible, or desirable, to refute every false position. Instead, we should concentrate on the correct one. Do this by asking the class to consider *only* what the *Bible* has to say.

I. A PROPER UNDERSTANDING.

We want to teach a simple, understandable lesson on Baptism. We must understand that it can only be administered by a proper authority, to proper subjects, for the proper purpose, by the proper mode.

A. The Proper Authority.

The word Baptize is used very loosely. Just as words like family, jury, and church can find meaning in special ways, the word Baptize is only meaningful when viewed in the proper context. Twelve people seated in a group do not constitute a jury. They must be impaneled by proper authority. A man, woman, and several children do not necessarily constitute a family. They may be total strangers who, by coincidence, are together in one location. Likewise, merely performing an act that looks like Baptism—even calling it Baptism—does not necessarily make that act Baptism. Proper authority for Baptism rests with the church—the local assembly of believers. Just as a jury must be properly impaneled, Baptism must be properly authorized. It should not be administered by the Parent-Teacher Association, or the Lions Club, or even by a well-intentioned individual. The commission to Baptize was given to the church, and can only be carried out by the authority of that assembly (Matt. 28:18–20).

B. The Proper Candidate.

The proper candidate for Baptism is a believer. In Acts 8:26–39, Philip is preaching to a man of Ethiopia. The man asked to be Baptized. "And Philip said, If thou believest with all thine heart, thou mayest. And he answered and said, I believe that Jesus Christ is the Son of God" (Acts 8:37).

Upon this confession of faith, they commanded the chariot to stand still. They went down into the water, both Philip and the Eunuch, and Philip Baptized this new believer. Notice that Baptism should only be administered to a person who believes with all his heart. Not just a head consent, but a heart belief is necessary. Otherwise, it is not Bible Baptism, but is merely an imitation. A person who is not a believer should not be Baptized. This fact, by itself, should show us that infants are not candidates for Baptism.

C. The Proper Purpose.

The proper purpose for Baptism is very important. Many people are Baptized for the remission of sins. They cling to a limited number of Scriptures which, when taken out of context, seem to teach that Baptism saves. They frustrate the clear teaching that we are saved by grace through faith, and not by works of righteousness (Eph. 2:8). Baptism is a work of righteousness. It does not get us saved or help us to get saved. Instead, it is an identification with our Saviour. "Therefore we are buried with him by baptism into death: that like as Christ was raised up from the dead by the glory of the Father, even so we also should walk in newness of life" (Rom. 6:4).

Baptism becomes our identifying mark with the death, burial, and resurrection of Jesus Christ.

D. The Proper Mode.

The word Baptize can find meaning in only one act—the act of immersion. There are several reasons why this is true. First, the word itself means to dip or plunge. Authorities on the Greek language are agreed. In the original language the word translated Baptize means immersion. Second, the words used to describe Baptism indicate immersion. In the case of Philip and the eunuch, *both* men went *down into* the water. The Baptism took place, then both men came *up out* of the water. Finally, Baptism is a symbol of the death, burial, and resurrection of Christ. This symbol is most fully presented by a candidate who is literally buried, or immersed, in water.

II. SOME IMPROPER CANDIDATES.

A. Those with Impure Hearts.

In Acts 8:5–24, there is the record of a man who was Baptized, but his heart was not right. He tried to buy the blessing of God with money. Peter rebuked him and said, "Thou hast neither part nor lot in this matter: for thy heart is not right in the sight of God" (Acts 8:21).

B. Those with Incomplete Message.

There were twelve men in Acts 19:1–7 who showed no evidence of salvation. They were disciples of John. They were not aware of the ministry, death, and resurrection of Christ. They had never heard of the Holy Spirit. Until they heard the complete message of Christ and received Him, they were not proper candidates for Baptism.

C. Those with Insincere Belief.

Constantine the Great, emperor of the Roman Empire, saw that Christians were of fine, noble character and decided that all the Roman Empire should be Christians. He had his armies

Baptized. These people, though they professed Christianity, were insincere. They were not believers, and therefore should not have been Baptized.

III. PROPER FOR OBEDIENCE.

Baptism is not essential for salvation, but it is essential for obedience to God (Matt. 28:19). Every believer should be baptized.

A. A Multitude.

On the day of Pentecost there were 3,000 converts. They were Baptized the same day (Acts 2:41).

B. A Eunuch.

The eunuch, led to the Lord by Philip, requested and received Baptism the same hour he was saved (Acts 8:36–38).

C. A Jailor.

The Philippian jailor, led to the Lord by Paul and Silas, was Baptized the same night (Acts 16:33).

CONCLUSION.

A proper understanding of the importance of Baptism is very important for every Christian. Baptism for the wrong reason can create false security. Failure to be Baptized is disobedience to God. The teacher should testify of his own Baptism, encouraging the students to follow Christ in this step of obedience. He should also determine if there are any in his class who are trusting in Baptism for salvation, and teach these the necessity of trusting in God's grace alone.

Reinforcing Illustrations:

1. The teacher should bring to class an employee identification card, preferably one with a picture of the employee. An organizational membership card may be substituted. This card illustrates Baptism in that: 1.) the carrier is identifying with the employer or organization. 2.) the card shows the employee's or member's willingness to obey leadership. 3.) the carrier of the card received it *because* he was an employee or member, not in order to *become* one.

2. Baptism is a picture. To illustrate this, the teacher may want to bring several pictures to class: a picture of a well-known person, perhaps the pastor or someone else whom the students can quickly identify; a photo or poster of an easily identified location or landmark. Point out that while the pictures are not the actual person or place, they do accurately show us what that person or place looks like. Whenever we see the picture, we immediately think of the person, place, or thing it represents.

Baptism pictures the death, burial, and resurrection of Jesus Christ. Whenever we see a Baptism, we ought to be immediately reminded that Jesus died, was buried, and rose again that we might have everlasting life.

3. On an elementary level, the teacher might bring several toys and personal items to class. Using a pen and paper labels, tags can be made showing to whom the items belong. The teacher should then ask the students to write their names in the fronts of their Bibles. Again, this shows ownership. Next, the teacher should make a label which says, "I belong to Jesus," and pin it on herself. Again, ownership is illustrated. Finally, the students should be told that there is an even better label that Christians can wear to show that they belong to Jesus. That label is Baptism.

4. For adults and older teens, the best illustration is that found in Rom. 6:4–6,11. When we accept Christ, the old man—our sinful nature—is reckoned to be dead. Dead things ought to be buried. In Baptism, the desire of the new Christian to bury, to put away forever, the spiritually dead nature is beautifully pictured. That which is dead is buried. That which is alive, the new nature, is resurrected. It will be wise to point out that people are buried because they are dead, not in order to make them dead. Challenge the students to visualize a funeral for the old nature. The dead corpse, with all the decay and ugliness that death brings, is put into the grave of water and forgotten. (Care should be taken to point out that Baptism *pictures* what God's attitude is and what our attitude ought to be toward the old nature—that it is dead and no longer in control. The final removal of this nature will not take place, of course, until the Christian receives his glorified body at Christ's return.)

Lesson Seven: Baptism
Lesson Text: Acts 8:38
Craft: Baptism Scene
Materials Needed:
  White paper: 1 sheet, 8½ x 11, per child
  Blue paper: 1 sheet, 4¼ x 11, per child
  Human figure: 1 per child cut from paper
  Paper fasteners: 1 per child
  Glue
Instructions:
  Prior to the session, trace and cut out the human figure and cut scallops along one edge of blue paper to resemble water. Each child should be given pieces of white and blue paper. The blue paper should be glued to the white paper on three sides, forming a pouch which is open at the scalloped edge. The human figure should be placed in the pouch. Press the paper fastener through both sheets of paper and through the feet of the figure. With the paper fastener as a pivot, the figure may be immersed in and removed from the water to illustrate Baptism.

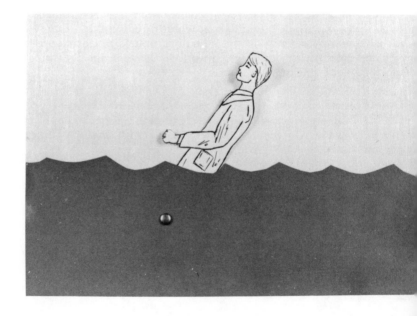

white

blue

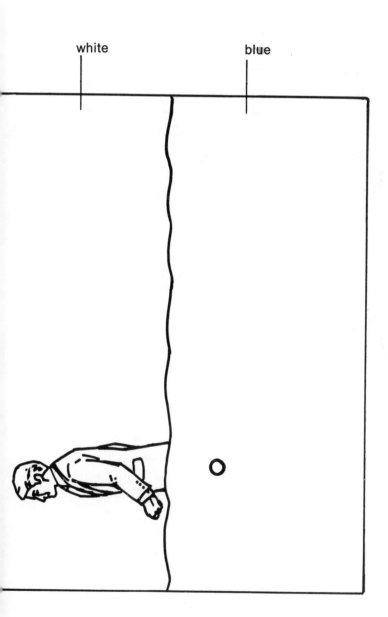

STUDY WORKSHEET

Lesson Seven—BAPTISM

PROPER UNDERSTANDING.

1. Proper authority for _____ rests with the church.

2. The proper _____ for Baptism is a _____.

3. Baptism is a work of _____; it is an _____ with the Saviour.

4. Baptism means to _____ or _____.

5. Baptism is a symbol of _____, _____, and _____.

6. Baptism is not essential for _____, but it is essential for _____.

Memory Verse: Therefore we are buried with him by baptism into death: that like as Christ was raised up from the dead by the glory of the Father, even so we also should walk in newness of life (Romans 6:4).

Short Version: Therefore we are buried with him by baptism.

FOUNDATIONAL BIBLE DOCTRINES

Lesson Seven—BAPTISM

PROPER UNDERSTANDING.

1. Proper authority for **Baptism** rests with the church.

2. The proper **candidate** for Baptism is a **believer**.

3. Baptism is a work of **righteousness**; it is an **identification** with the Saviour.

4. Baptism means to **dip** or **plunge**.

5. Baptism is a symbol of **death**, **burial**, and **resurrection**.

6. Baptism is not essential for **salvation**, but it is essential for **obedience**.

Memory Verse: Therefore we are buried with him by baptism into death: that like as Christ was raised up from the dead by the glory of the Father, even so we also should walk in newness of life (Romans 6:4).

Short Version: Therefore we are buried with him by baptism.

FOUNDATIONAL BIBLE DOCTRINES

A. V. Henderson, Pastor, Temple Baptist Church
Detroit, Michigan

Lesson Eight—The Lord's Supper

INTRODUCTION.
I. GOD'S MEMORIALS.
    A. The Passover.
    B. The Jar of Manna.
    C. The Twelve Stones.
    D. The Anointing at Bethany.
II. GOD'S MEMORIAL SUPPER.
    A. The Last Passover.
    B. The Broken Body.
    C. The Shed Blood.
    D. The Coming Kingdom.
    E. The Personal Examination.
    F. The Proper Administration.
CONCLUSION.

References for Study:
    Ex. 12; 16:12–32; Josh. 4:1–8; Matt. 26:6–13,17–30; 1 Cor. 11:20–30.

Memory Verse:
    But let a man examine himself, and so let him eat of that bread, and drink of that cup (1 Cor. 11:28).

Aim:
    To establish once and for all the clear teaching of this ordinance.

Point of Contact:
    Have your students engage in some memory exercise to demonstrate how forgetful people are. You may ask them to describe what one member of the class wore to church the week before, or to name the presidents of the United States, or quote the preamble to the Constitution. You may ask them to tie a string around their finger as a reminder to do something.

INTRODUCTION.
    Memory is important. There are many things which we ought to remember. Some we must remember, while others we choose to remember. We leave ourselves notes or mark on a

calendar things we should remember to do. We save newspaper clippings of or build memorials to things or people we want to remember. In fact, the word memorial comes from the word memory. A memorial is something which stirs our memory of a past event.

I. GOD'S MEMORIALS.

God knows how forgetful we are, so He sets things in our way to cause us to remember. He establishes memorials to call to our mind important truths.

A. The Passover.

In Exodus 12, the Hebrews ate an unusual meal. They had been captives in Egypt for centuries, yet God now promised deliverance. Through His servant Moses, He specifically outlined this unusual feast, the Passover. The children of Israel were to kill a lamb, to sprinkle its blood above the door, and to eat the lamb. They were to eat it while fully dressed for a long journey. That night God's Death Angel passed over Egypt, killing the firstborn of every house not displaying the blood above the door. Stricken with fear, the Pharaoh and people allowed the Hebrews to leave the country. In fact, they drove them out. Though they were free from Egypt, the supper was instituted as an annual feast for a memorial. God told His people that the time would come when the children would ask, "What mean ye by this service?" (Ex. 12:26). Then the elders could teach the younger folks about the Passover and preserve the memory of it.

B. The Jar of Manna.

In Exodus 16, God fed these same people, during their wilderness journey, with bread from Heaven. The people of God called it manna. The taste of it was like wafers made with honey. God wanted people to remember His ability to care for His own, so He commanded, "Fill an omer of it to be kept for your generations; that they may see the bread wherewith I have fed you in the wilderness, when I brought you forth from the land of Egypt" (Ex. 16:32). This bread was preserved from one generation to another as a gentle reminder of God's ability to prepare a table even in the wilderness.

C. The Twelve Stones.

In Joshua 4, the people of God readied themselves to cross the Jordan River into the Promised Land. From each of the twelve tribes, Joshua chose one man for a special chore. These twelve men were to bring a stone from the bed of the Jordan and set them together for an altar unto the Lord. These stones could not yet be seen, because they were hidden beneath the waters of the river. But when the waters were cut off by the hand of God, they were revealed and carried forth. God had a very special purpose for this altar of stones taken miraculously from the bed of the Jordan. He told Joshua: "That this may be a sign among you, that when your children ask their fathers in time to come, saying, what mean ye by these stones?" (Josh. 4:6). Then this memory aid could be used to tell how God opened the flood waters for His own.

D. The Anointing Ointment.

In Matthew 26, there is a record of the anointing of Jesus by a woman of Bethany. Her action represented not only affection, but insight and sacrifice. It showed insight, in that she realized who Christ was and the importance of His ministry. It showed sacrifice, in that the ointment was valuable and would not ordinarily be so lavishly used. Not wanting the world to forget this woman's act of dedication, Jesus said, "Wheresoever this gospel shall be preached in the whole world, there shall also this, that this woman hath done, be told for a memorial of her" (Matt. 26:13).

II. GOD'S MEMORIAL SUPPER.

In our time God has provided an ordinance that prompts the memory. It is called "The Lord's Supper." ". . . this do in remembrance of me" (1 Cor. 11:24).

A. The Last Passover.

Jesus was with His disciples in a borrowed upper room when He instituted this new supper (Matt. 26:17–30). It was the time of the Passover, mentioned earlier. The original Passover had been both a memorial of God's liberation of Israel from the bonds of Egypt and a prophecy of the coming of another sacrificial lamb—Jesus Christ. As He met with His disciples, Jesus celebrated the final Passover, for the following day He fulfilled the prophetic aspect of that feast when He died on Cavalry as the Lamb who would take away the sins of the world.

B. The Broken Body.

Jesus instituted this new memorial service by taking a piece of bread and giving thanks for it. Then He broke it and distributed it among His disciples saying, "Take, eat; this is my body" (Matt. 26:26). The eating of this broken bread is to remind us of His broken body. It is a memorial to Christ's sacrificial death. "This do in remembrance of me" (1 Cor. 11:24).

C. The Shed Blood.

Next Jesus took the cup, gave thanks, and gave it to the disciples, saying, "Drink ye all of it; for this is my blood of the new testament, which is shed for many for the remission of sins" (Matt. 26:27,28). Here the memorial not only reminds, but teaches. For it is not merely by Christ's death that remission of sins is given. He shed His blood that our sins might be forgiven. So, this memorial supper will constantly remind us that Christ literally poured out His blood so that we might be saved.

D. The Coming Kingdom.

This memorial service, like the Passover, is also a prophecy. It looks forward to the time when Jesus promised to drink the cup with us anew in the Father's Kingdom (Matt. 26:29). As the Passover prophesied His death, the Lord's Supper prophesies His return to reign as King.

E. The Personal Examination.

This memorial service that looks back to the death of Jesus and forward to His second coming, also has a bearing on the present. As we partake of this supper, we are bidden to examine ourselves and sit in judgment on those things which are wrong (1 Cor. 11:28).

F. The Proper Administration.

The New Testament church is the custodian and administrator of this feast, and it should not be administered to satisfy hunger, but to call us to memory (1 Cor. 11:20–22).

CONCLUSION.

Men are prone to forget. We forget everything from addresses to anniversaries. But we cannot afford to forget some things. The Lord's sacrificial death is one of those things. A proper understanding of this ordinance will always keep in front of us this very important event. The teacher may use this opportunity to teach salvation through this memorial to Christ's sacrifice.

Reinforcing Illustrations:

1. The teacher may bring photos or magazine clippings of famous monuments or memorials to class. As the pictures, are shown, the pupils should be challenged to guess of what each memorial is a reminder. Finally, the teacher should show a picture representing the Lord's Supper—bread, cup, people observing the Lord's Supper—and ask what this act memorializes. This exercise could also be carried out orally.

2. The teacher may ask if any pupil was named after another person—an uncle, cousin, father, or friend. By bearing another's name, the pupil is a type of memorial.

3. A memorial card may be obtained from a funeral home and the name of Jesus Christ and the dates of His birth, death,

and resurrection written inside. As the card is passed among the pupils, the teacher can explain that there is another memorial to Christ's death—the Lord's Supper. Care should be taken here to point out that unlike mortal man, Christ is not dead but risen and living in Heaven.

4. Everyone has received a report card at one time or another. Mimeograph report cards for the students. Areas of evaluation should include: prayer, Bible reading, witnessing, obedience to God, submission to authority, attitude, patience, kindness, or any others the teacher feels are appropriate. Tell the students that, for a change, they may grade themselves. But remind them that God will know whether their self-evaluation is honest. Ask them to carefully study the areas in which they scored poorly. Encourage them to seek forgiveness where necessary, and challenge them to improve their "grade" in the future. This is exactly the process every Christian should follow before receiving the Lord's Supper. They may not use an actual report card each time, but this spiritual evaluation should always be a part of the celebration of this ordinance.

Lesson Eight: The Lord's Supper
Lesson Text: Matt. 26:26
Craft: Lord's Supper Carry Home
Materials Needed:
   Light brown or blue construction paper for background
   Golden brown (yellow) construction paper for bread shapes
   Blue or gold construction paper for cup or chalice
   Glue
Instructions:
   Using the patterns provided, cut out shapes to represent one
piece of bread and one cup for each child. These should be cut
on a fold so that they are double and will open after gluing. The
children can be allowed to color the background to represent
wood, as on a table top. The shapes should then be attached.
Inside each should be pasted a copy of the verse portion appro-
priately identifying the symbols of the Lord's Supper. (The
verse portions can be written in if necessary.)

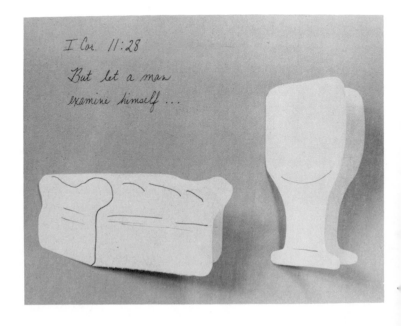

cup

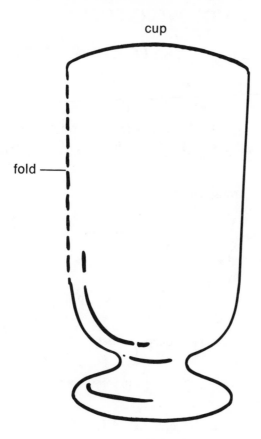

fold

cut double — glue one side
down to allow other to open
as a door

fold

bread

STUDY WORKSHEET

Lesson Eight—THE LORD'S SUPPER

GOD'S MEMORIALS.

1. In observance of the _____ the Jews killed a lamb and sprinkled the _____ on the doorpost (Exodus 12:26).

2. The bread from Heaven was called _____ (Exodus 16:32).

3. Stones were brought to build an _____ unto the Lord (Joshua 4:6).

4. The anointing oil showed _____ and _____ (Matthew 26:6–13).

GOD'S MEMORIAL SUPPER.

1. Jesus and the _____ celebrated the last _____ (Matthew 26:17–30).

2. The broken bread symbolizes Christ's broken _____ (Matthew 26:26).

3. He shed His _____ so our sins might be forgiven (Matthew 26:28).

4. The Lord's Supper prophesies His return to reign as _____. (Matthew 26:29).

5. We are bidden to _____ ourselves (1 Corinthians 11:28).

6. The _____ is to administer communion.

Memory Verse: But let a man examine himself, and so let him eat of that bread, and drink of that cup (1 Corinthians 11:28).

FOUNDATIONAL BIBLE DOCTRINES

Lesson Eight—THE LORD'S SUPPER

GOD'S MEMORIALS.

1. In observance of the **Passover** the Jews killed a lamb and sprinkled the **blood** on the doorpost (Exodus 12:26).
2. The bread from Heaven was called **manna** (Exodus 16:32).
3. Stones were brought to build an **altar** unto the Lord (Joshua 4:6).
4. The anointing oil showed **affection** and **sacrifice** (Matthew 26:6–13).

GOD'S MEMORIAL SUPPER.

1. Jesus and the **disciples** celebrated the last **supper** (Matthew 26:17–30).
2. The broken bread symbolizes Christ's broken **body** (Matthew 26:26).
3. He shed His **blood** so our sins might be forgiven (Matthew 26:28).
4. The Lord's Supper prophesies His return to reign as **King** (Matthew 26:29).
5. We are bidden to **examine** ourselves (1 Corinthians 11:28).
6. The **church** is to administer communion.

Memory Verse: But let a man examine himself, and so let him eat of that bread, and drink of that cup (1 Corinthians 11:28).

FOUNDATIONAL BIBLE DOCTRINES

Jack Hyles, Pastor, First Baptist Church
Hammond, Indiana

Lesson Nine—The Church

INTRODUCTION.
  I. THE DEFINITION OF THE CHURCH.
     A. The Church Now.
     B. The Church Later.
     C. The Church Mistaken.
  II. THE STRUCTURE OF THE CHURCH.
  III. THE PURPOSES OF THE CHURCH.
     A. Soul-winning and Baptizing.
     B. Doctrinal Study.
     C. Fellowship.
     D. Sitting at the Lord's Table.
     E. Giving.
     F. Praise.
     G. Continuing in Soul-winning.
  IV. OBLIGATIONS TO THE CHURCH.
     A. Attendance.
     B. Stewardship.
     C. Loyalty.
     D. Dedication.
  V. EXAMPLES.
CONCLUSION.

References for Study:
    Matt. 16:18; Luke 4:16; Acts 2:41–47; 7:38; 13:1–3; 19:32,39; 1 Cor. 1:10,11; 6:14–16,19,20; 16:2; Phil. 1:1,25,26; 2:18; Heb. 10:25; 12:23; Rev. 2:1–5,8–17; 3:1,2,7–22.

Memory Verse:
    Not forsaking the assembling of ourselves together, as the manner of some is; but exhorting one another: and so much the more, as ye see the day approaching (Heb. 10:25).

Aim:
    To teach the pupils the importance of the Church in their lives.

Point of Contact:
    As the pupils enter the class, give each a small pencil and piece of paper. Give them 60 seconds to list the names of as

many churches as they can. Give them another 60 seconds to list the names of as many pastors as possible. Then give them another 60 seconds to list as many deacons of the Church as come to their minds. Perhaps the one who lists the most of each could receive some small prize—a small book from the bookstore, or a gospel pin, or a Scripture-text ballpoint pen would be splendid gifts for such prizes. On the elementary level the point of contact could be used by children giving verbal answers to the questions.

INTRODUCTION.

The doctrine of the Church is an important doctrine, an intricate one, and one that is often misunderstood. In a limited time, we will not be able to explore all the depths of the subject, nor will we consider fully such tantalizing aspects as the date of the founding of the Church. We will give a simple, yet concise, picture of what the Bible says about the Church, its structure, its operation, and its importance in the lives of individual Christians.

I. THE DEFINITION OF THE CHURCH.
A. *The Church Now.*

The word translated "Church" comes from two Greek words—ek, which means "out of," and kaleo (call-eh-o), which means "a calling." The word was used among the Greeks of a body of people who gathered for secular reasons in Acts 19:39. It is also used concerning Israel in Acts 7:38. It is used concerning a riotous mob in Acts 19:32,41. This leads us to the conclusion that a church is a called-out assembly. The New Testament Church is a called-out assembly of believers. Hence, for this age the term "Churches" would be more appropriate than the term "Church."

A New Testament Church is a local group of called-out believers who assemble on a scriptural basis for the carrying out of God's commands and commission and for the providing of fellowship, strength, encouragement, edification, and Christian growth to God's people. It is vital that every Christian align himself with such a Church in order that he may participate in the two-fold ministry of being strengthened and strengthening.

B. *The Church Later.*

There is another sense in which the Church is mentioned in the Bible. Passages such as Heb. 12:23 tell us that there is a Church being formed now that will be completed at the rapture. This is perhaps the Church mentioned in Matt. 16:18. It must be noticed, however, that when our Lord spoke the words, "I will build my church," this is the durative or linear which means, "I will be building my Church." Perhaps it could be better translated, "I will be building and be building and be building my Church." He will continue in this building until the last person is saved and the bride is called out. Then, and not until then, will all believers become a Church, for then, and not until then, will they be a called-out assembly.

Suppose a pastor is taking some out-of-town guests on a tour of his Church property. The Church is in a building program. The pastor drives by the building site, points to the unfinished building and says, "That's our Church building." Now, though they understand what he is saying, he does not mean exactly what he is saying. What he means is that there is a Church building that is being built. It is not yet a Church building. It has not yet been finished or dedicated. Some passages seem to teach us that the word Church is used about this unfinished body of Christ, but until it is a called-out assembly at the meeting in the air, it will not be a Church.

There is a great danger for people to misunderstand this doctrine, causing them to bypass the called-out assembly that God has provided for us here. Many are weak in the faith and unfruitful in their service for Christ because they have bypassed the local assembly, thinking that it is trivial or at best, a nursery for young Christians.

C. The Church Mistaken.

Often God's people mistakenly refer to a building as a Church. It is true that in early Bible days God's presence was peculiarly manifested in a building. From the altar of the days of the partriarchs to the tabernacle of the traveling Israelites to the temple of the Jews, God seemed to dwell in a certain place in a special way. However, in this age the body of the believer is the temple of the Holy Spirit, as is found in 1 Cor. 6:14–16, 19, 20. Perhaps the thoughtful teacher would want to secure pictures of the Church building, of an individual Christian, and of a group picture of the Church family. The teacher could hold the picture of the Church building in front of the class and ask them what they see. The answer, of course, is that they see a Church building. It should be emphasized this is not the Church but simply a meeting place. Then, the picture of the individual Christian could be held up and the pupils would be asked, "What is this?" The answer is that this is a Christian whose body is the temple of the Holy Spirit. Then the picture of the Church family could be held up and the pupils are asked, "And what is this?" The correct answer is, "This is our Church."

II. THE STRUCTURE OF THE CHURCH.

This is outlined very plainly in Phil. 1:1. Even the casual observer will notice that there are three groups mentioned concerning the Church structure: saints, pastors, and deacons.

There are three titles given to the pastors. First is the word "pastor" which means "shepherd" which means that God has given to the pastor the watch-care of the flock (saints). Second is the word "bishop" which means "overseer." The pastor is to be the overseer of the entire Church program. This does not mean he is to be the dictator, but it means that he is to oversee the total ministry of the Church. Third, the pastor is called an "elder." This points to wisdom, counsel, and advice, which every faithful pastor owes to his people.

The deacons of the Church are servants chosen because of the heavy load that the pastor carries. They are his helpers to help him carry the responsibilities and burdens of the Church. Under no condition are they his bosses. Many Churches have found it wise to form the deacons into an advisory board to work with the pastor in prayerfully seeking God's will concerning the Church and its ministry, enabling them to make proper recommendations to the Church concerning the Lord's work.

III. THE PURPOSES OF THE CHURCH.

Acts. 2:41–47. Notice the program carried out by this typical, healthy Church at Jerusalem.

    A. Soul-winning and baptizing. Verse 41.
    B. Doctrinal Study. Verse 42a.
    C. Fellowship. Verse 42b.
    D. Sitting at the Lord's table. Verse 42c.
    E. Giving. Verse 45.
    F. Praise. Verse 47a.
    G. Continuing in soul-winning. Verse 47b.

These are just a few of the wonderful things that the Church offers to God's people for their growth in grace.

IV. OBLIGATIONS TO THE CHURCH.

When a person becomes a member of a local assembly he assumes some obligations. Some of these are:

A. Attendance.

Read Heb. 10:25. Every Christian should be faithful to all the public services of his Church. One of the sweetest passages concerning the life of our Lord is Luke 4:16, "And He came to Nazareth, where he had been brought up: and, as his custom was, he went into the synagogue on the sabbath day, and stood up for to read." Though there was no New Testament Church when Jesus was a lad, He nevertheless was faithful to the synagogue. How much more faithful should we be to the New Testament Church founded by our Lord Himself!

B. Stewardship of our Possessions.

1 Cor. 16:2 teaches us that we are to bring our monetary gifts on the first day of the week. Since the first day of the week was the day that the New Testament Church met for fellowship, the apostle was no doubt talking about our bringing tithes and offerings to Church with us as we come.

C. Loyalty.

D. Dedication.

The Christian, especially the Christian child or young person, should build his life around his Church. His social activities should be Church-centered. His closest friends should be from his Church. His dates should be chosen from the young people at Church, and whenever it is possible, he should attend a school operated by his Church.

V. EXAMPLES.

There are many Churches or assemblies mentioned in the Bible. It might be wise for us to learn five of the good Churches and five of the bad and at least one characteristic about each: (1) The Church at Jerusalem was the first New Testament Church (Acts 2:47). (2) The Church at Antioch sent out the first missionaries (Acts 13:1–3). (3) The Church at Philadelphia was the Church of brotherly love (Rev. 3:7–13). (4) The Church at Smyrna was a suffering Church (Rev. 2:8–11). (5) The Church at Philippi was a joyful Church (Phil. 1:25,26; 2:18). (6) The Church at Laodicea was a lukewarm Church (Rev. 3:14–22). (7) The Church at Corinth was a divided Church (1 Cor. 1:10,11). (8) The Church at Pergamos was a worldly Church (Rev. 2:12–17). (9) The Church at Ephesus was a Church that had left its first love (Rev. 2:1–5). (10) The Church at Sardis was a dead Church (Rev. 3:1,2).

CONCLUSION.

The teacher should testify for 60 seconds or so concerning what his Church means to him. He should mention such things as he was saved, baptized, met his best friends, met his mate for life, was married, surrendered his life in a special way, etc. Teacher, ask God at this point to make your heart warm as you seek to influence your pupils to realize the importance of their Church in their lives.

Reinforcing Illustrations:

1. Ask each class member to write a note of appreciation to a pastor or a deacon or a special member of the Church that has been a blessing.

2. Hold a white sheet of paper in front of the class. Take a

crayon or a magic marker and make a bold dot in the middle of the paper. Ask the class what they see. Of course, the answer will be, "I see a dot." Remind the class that that is what causes trouble in Churches. Nothing was said about the white surrounding the dot. Most of the paper is white, but all we see is the dot.

3. On the elementary level, the teacher could bring some toy soldiers to class. Let one soldier represent a Christian. Remind the class that this soldier, in order to be effective in battle, must join the other soldiers. Though he belongs to the army, his usefulness depends on his association with his own outfit, regiment, battalion, company, platoon, squad. The same is true with the child of God. Though he belongs to Christ, he nevertheless needs to join himself to the fighting unit—the local assembly of believers which we call the New Testament Church.

4. Have a pupil act out silently something that we do in Church. See which class member can guess first what he is doing. The class member could act out fellowship by shaking hands, the Lord's Supper by acting like he is drinking and eating, baptism, giving an offering, preaching, etc.

5. Have each member choose a particular pastor and/or deacon, write his name in the flyleaf of his Bible, and pray for him in a special way the next week.

6. List the ten Churches previously mentioned. Beside them list their characteristics. Have the pupils match the characteristic to the Church.

1. Jerusalem		a.	Worldly
2. Antioch		b.	First established
3. Philadelphia		c.	Suffering
4. Smyrna		d.	Joyful
5. Philippi		e.	Dead
6. Laodicea		f.	Divided
7. Corinth		g.	First missionary
8. Pergamos		h.	Lukewarm
9. Ephesus		i.	Loving
10. Sardis		j.	Left first love

Lesson Nine: The Church
Lesson Text: Matt. 16:18
Craft: Church with Stained Glass Window

Materials used:

Church shapes cut from any color construction paper (2 per child)
Razor blade
Glue (mixed with equal parts water)
Small brushes
Several colors of tissue paper cut in sheets of approximately 2 ft. sq. for easy handling
Wax paper

Instructions:

Before the class session, cut Church shapes from construction paper. Using the razor blade, cut large window shapes in the center of each Church shape.

Prepare the glue mixture and put glue, tissue paper, brush, and one piece of wax paper (12" X 12") per child on each table.

To make the "stained glass," rub glue solution on the center of the wax paper. Tear (don't cut) small pieces of tissue paper from the various colors provided; place these one at a time in the glue already on the wax paper being sure to flatten them and remove any creases. With the brush coat this and each successive piece of tissue paper, allowing pieces to overlap to form varying shades and colors. After enough tissue paper is in place to fill the window shape, apply a final coat of glue and allow this to dry. The tissue paper design may be peeled from the wax paper or simply cut (approximately ½" larger) to fit between the two pieces forming the Church and filling the window cut out. Hang this in a window to allow light to pass through. The text may be written on the Church design.

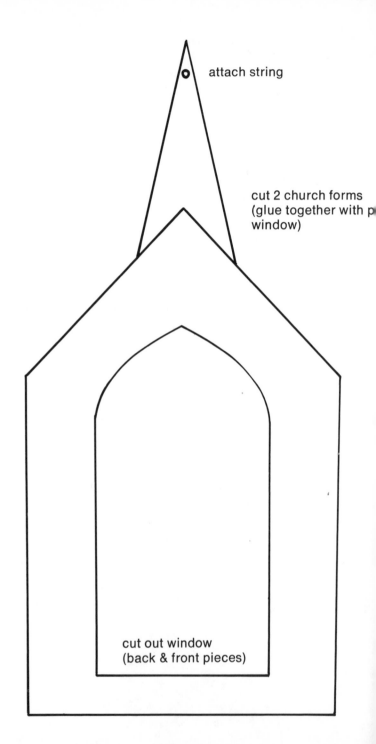

attach string

cut 2 church forms
(glue together with p
window)

cut out window
(back & front pieces)

STUDY WORKSHEET

Lesson Nine—THE CHURCH

THE DEFINITION OF THE CHURCH.

1. The Church is a _____ assembly of believers.

2. The Church is not a _____. It is _____.

THE STRUCTURE OF THE CHURCH.

1. The _____ is a "Shepherd."

2. The _____ are chosen servants.

Five Purposes of a Church are: _____, _____,
_____, _____, and _____ (Acts 2:41–47).

Obligations to the Church: _____, _____, _____,
_____.

Memory Verse: Not forsaking the assembling of ourselves together, as the manner of some is; but exhorting one another: and so much the more, as ye see the day approaching (Hebrews 10:25).

Short Version: Not forsaking the assembling of ourselves together.

FOUNDATIONAL BIBLE DOCTRINES

Lesson Nine—THE CHURCH

THE DEFINITION OF THE CHURCH.

1. The Church is a **called out** assembly of believers.

2. The Church is not a **building**. It is **people**.

THE STRUCTURE OF THE CHURCH.

1. The **pastor** is a "Shepherd."

2. The **deacons** are chosen servants.

   Five Purposes of a Church are: **Soul-winning**, **fellowship**, **praise**, **study**, and **giving** (Acts 2:41–47).

   Obligations to the Church: **attendance**, **stewardship**, **loyalty**, **dedication**.

Memory Verse: Not forsaking the assembling of ourselves together, as the manner of some is; but exhorting one another: and so much the more, as ye see the day approaching (Hebrews 10:25).

Short Version: Not forsaking the assembling of ourselves together.

FOUNDATIONAL BIBLE DOCTRINES

A. V. Henderson, Pastor, Temple Baptist Church
Detroit, Michigan

Lesson Ten—Separation

INTRODUCTION.
I. THE AUTHOR OF SEPARATION.
   A. Instances of Separation.
   B. Interpretation of Separation
II. THE COMMAND OF SEPARATION.
   A. Put Away Darkness.
   B. Not Unequally Yoked.
   C. Come Out.
III. THE CHARACTER OF SEPARATION.
   A. The Two Aspects.
   B. The Results.
CONCLUSION.

References for Study:
   Gen. 1:4; Deut. 22:9–11; Matt. 13:24–30,36–43; John 17:15; Rom. 1:1; 12:1,2; 13:12–14; 1 Cor. 9:7–10; 2 Cor. 6:14–18; 7:1.

Memory Verse:
   And be not conformed to this world: but be ye transformed by the renewing of your mind, that ye may prove what is that good, and acceptable, and perfect, will of God (Rom. 12:2).

Aim:
   To set forth in a simple way the great doctrine of personal sanctification.

Point of Contact:
   Mix together some objects that obviously do not belong together. Then have your pupils separate them, stating how the objects differ.

INTRODUCTION.
   A close study of the Scriptures is necessary on this most important topic, because people tend to substitute personal conviction for scriptural truth. We do not wish to suppress personal conviction, we want to encourage it; but don't expect everyone to share your convictions unless they can be backed up with a chapter and verse reference.

I. THE AUTHOR OF SEPARATION.

A. Instances of Separation.

In the opening of the Bible, we see God dividing the light from the darkness. "And God saw the light, that it was good: and God divided the light from the darkness" (Gen. 1:4). God, by example, is demonstrating to us that many things must be divided or separated one from the other. Some things, by their very nature, cannot be mixed. The moment light appears, it is no longer dark. And darkness, by definition, is the absence of light. There cannot be one where the other exists. This truth may seem too elementary to be given much thought, but it is, as we will see, a truth to which Scripture calls to our attention over and over again.

God also required a division or separation of seeds sown in a vineyard. "Thou shalt not sow thy vineyard with diverse seeds: lest the fruit of thy seed which thou hast sown, and the fruit of thy vineyard, be defiled" (Deut. 22:9). Once the seeds were sown together, they became so mixed that the fruit was not pure. Once sown, it is nearly impossible to separate the two. This is a major lesson in the parable of the wheat and the tares found in Matt. 13:24–30, 36–43. Had the field been allowed to yield only wheat, there would have been no doubt as to the nature of each plant. But once the field became defiled with the seeds of tares, once the separation had broken down, it became difficult to tell the two types of plants apart. Of course, this is not the only truth taught in this parable, but it is an important principle and worthy of our attention. God forbade the sowing of the seeds together because of ineptitude.

The beasts of burden that worked in the fields were to be separated. "Thou shalt not plow with an ox and an ass together" (Deut. 22:10). This is a case of incompatibility. The very nature of these two animals forbids that they work together. They have a different gait and differ in strength. They cannot work together comfortably.

There were even different kinds of garments that God did not allow His people to wear together. "Thou shalt not wear a garment of divers sorts, as of woolen and linen together" (Deut. 22:11), a case of inharmony.

B. Interpretation of Separation.

What was the purpose in God's clear declaration that different things are to be separated? Was His primary concern for the literal fruits of the vineyard, or for the actual ox and ass, or for the unharmonious mixing of fabrics. Paul explains the hidden principle behind ceremonial law in 1 Cor. 9:7–10. God outlined ceremonial law as a picture, a constant reminder, of moral truth. God demanded the separation of seeds and animals and garments; He separated light from darkness, to illustrate to men that things which are different in basic nature ought to be separate. Men who live in spiritual darkness cannot mix well with men who live in spiritual light. When seeds of spiritual impurity are sown among good seeds, it becomes difficult to distinguish the spiritual wheat from the tares. The distinct quality and testimony of the good is swallowed up and hidden among the bad. Animals of different strength, size, and temperament do not work together well. They are not suited to the same things. Nor are the activities of the world suited to the life-style of the Christian. When God commanded His people not to blend certain fabrics and garments, He was teaching, in principle, that His people should also not blend those things which are godly with those things that are ungodly. It is the responsibility of God's people to be as easily distinguished from the world as light is from darkness, not to be so mixed among the tares that only final harvest can separate the two.

II. THE COMMAND OF SEPARATION.
A. Put Away Darkness.
God does not stop with teaching Separation by example. He commands that Christians live a life that is separated from the conduct of the world. Paul, writing in Rom. 13:12–14, says that Christians are to cast off darkness and put on the armor of light. He is speaking to the saved in these verses, and not to those who are lost. He is telling Christians that they must be separate from the works of darkness. They are not to be identified with the activities of the world. They are to cast them away and make no provision for them.

B. Not Unequally Yoked.
In 2 Cor. 6:14 the believer is commanded not to be yoked with unbelievers. A yoke is an implement of work, and the Christian's work of glorifying Christ is totally alien to the unbeliever. It is contrary to the unbeliever's nature to glorify the Son of God. So, if the believer and unbeliever are working together, their work will probably not be the kind that brings glory to Christ Jesus. Of course, we do not mean that the saved and lost cannot work together in the sense of working for the same employer. When we speak of work, we are speaking of the motivation or thrust of an individual's life. That motivation, for the Christian, is to bring glory to the Father and to His Son. The unbeliever will only bring glory to himself.

C. Come Out.
God's clear command is to come out from among unbelievers. See 2 Cor. 6:14–18. Again, we are not to sever all connections with unbelievers. We cannot win those to Christ with whom we have no contact at all. But, we are not to identify with

them. Our goals are to differ from their goals. Our motivations are to differ from their motivations. Our activities are to differ from their activities. Our attitudes are to differ from their attitudes. Believers are to be identifiably different from unbelievers. God commands it.

III. THE CHARACTER OF SEPARATION.

A. The Two Aspects of Separation.

As we have seen, Bible Separation is not withdrawing physically from the world. Jesus, in John 17:15, prayed not that believers should be taken out of the world, only that they should be kept from the evil of the world. Nor is Separation simply avoiding those questionable or sinful activities that are common among the unsaved. True, Scripture says that we should so separate ourselves from worldly activity that we do not even make provision for the lust of our flesh. However, there is more to Separation than a negative list of things not to do. Bible Separation means also being separated, or set apart, to God. This is taught in Rom. 1:1. The same passage in Rom. 13:12–14 that told us earlier to cast off the works of darkness now tells us to put on the armor of light. It also tells us to put on Jesus Christ. We are to give the living of our lives over to Christ. His word and the working of His Holy Spirit are to be the center of our lives. Separation has two aspects: the putting off of the things of the world and the putting on of the power and grace of Jesus Christ. We are to make Him Lord of our lives, to fully submit and surrender to His perfect will (Rom. 12:1,2). This is the final goal of Separation, dedicating ourselves fully to Him.

B. The Results of Separation.

The reward for Bible Separation is fellowship with the Father. Read carefully the words of 2 Cor. 6:14–18. Righteousness has no fellowship with unrighteousness. Light has no communion with darkness. Christ has no concord, or agreement, with Belial. The believer has no part with the infidel. God's temple, the believer, has no agreement with the temple of idols. But God's command is not without promise. He tells us that if we will separate ourselves from these things, He will receive us, fellowship with us, and be to us as a Father is to sons and daughters. The fellowship and blessing of God depend upon our practicing Bible Separation.

CONCLUSION.

The promise of God's fellowship should motivate us to true Bible Separation. "Having therefore these promises dearly beloved, let us cleanse ourselves from all filthiness of the flesh and spirit, perfecting holiness in the fear of God" (2 Cor. 7:1).

Reinforcing Illustrations:

1. The teacher may partially fill a clear drinking glass with water. Light lubricating oil should be poured on top of the water. Though the two may mix together for a moment, the oil will soon separate itself from the water by rising to the surface. Likewise, the saved may temporarily mix with the lost, but the different natures of the two will cause them to separate.

2. A favorite illustration with children involves a walnut and some beans. Place a walnut, still in the shell, in the bottom of an empty jar. Fill the jar half-full of uncooked beans and screw on the cap. Shake the jar vigorously. In a few moments the walnut will appear on top of all the beans. Turn the jar over and shake it again. The result will always be the same. The beans and walnut are different. They will always separate.

3. Ask two students to stand on opposite sides of the room. One will represent Christ, while the other will represent the world. Ask a third student to stand half-way between the two. As he walks closer to the world, he must get further and further away from the student representing Christ. If he draws closer to Christ, he will naturally get further and further from the world. This illustrates the two aspects of separation, being separated from the world and being separated to Christ.

4. Ask the class to imagine an experiment in which two men are fed different diets. One receives a nourishing diet of meat and vegetables—all that he wants. The other is given a limited supply of bread and water. Which will be healthier? The one with the nourishing diet, of course. Likewise, if we separate our spiritual nature from godly influences and feed our sin nature on worldly things, our flesh will be strong and our spirit weak. If we separate our carnal nature from worldly things and feed our spiritual nature on the things of Christ, we will have good spiritual health.

Lesson Ten: Separation
Lesson Text: Matt. 5:16a
Craft: Candle plaque
Materials Needed:
    Felt—gold, blue, red
    Construction paper—white, yellow, brown
    Glue
Instructions:
    In advance, cut out shapes for:
        Flame—yellow construction paper
        Candle—white construction paper
        Base—gold, blue, or red felt

Hand out to the children light brown construction paper. Let them glue the pieces of the candle onto the construction paper. When completed, have them sing "This Little Light of Mine." You may also write the memory verse under the base of the candle.

Let your light so shine before men.   Matt. 5:16a

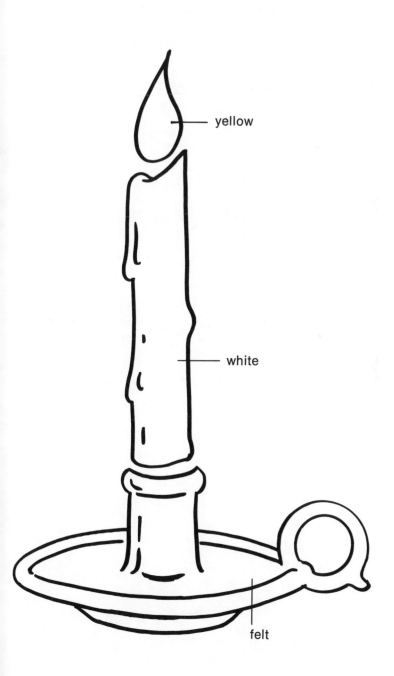

yellow

white

felt

119

STUDY WORKSHEET

Lesson Ten—SEPARATION

Darkness and _____ cannot mix.

THE COMMAND OF SEPARATION.

1. Cast off _____ put on _____ (Romans 13:12–14).

2. Be not unequally _____ with unbelievers (2 Corinthians 6:14).

3. Come out from among them and be ye _____.

CHARACTER OF SEPARATION.

1. We are to be separated from the _____, and to _____ (Romans 1:1).

2. Separation will result in _____ with the Father (2 Corinthians 16:14–18).

Memory Verse: And be not conformed to this world: but be ye transformed by the renewing of your mind, that ye may prove what is that good, and acceptable, and perfect, will of God (Romans 12:2).

Short Version: Be not conformed . . . but be ye transformed.

FOUNDATIONAL BIBLE DOCTRINES

Lesson Ten—SEPARATION

Darkness and **light** cannot mix.

THE COMMAND OF SEPARATION.

1. Cast off **darkness** put on **light** (Romans 13:12–14).

2. Be not unequally **yoked** with unbelievers (2 Corinthians 6:14).

3. Come out from among them and be ye **separate.**

CHARACTER OF SEPARATION.

1. We are to be separated from the **world**, and to **God** (Romans 1:1).

2. Separation will result in **fellowship** with the Father (2 Corinthians 6:14–18).

Memory Verse: And be not conformed to this world: but be ye transformed by the renewing of your mind, that ye may prove what is that good, and acceptable, and perfect, will of God (Romans 12:2).

Short Version: Be not conformed . . . but be ye transformed.

FOUNDATIONAL BIBLE DOCTRINES

Jerry Falwell, Pastor, Thomas Road Baptist Church
Lynchburg, Virginia

Lesson Eleven—Heaven

INTRODUCTION.
  I. THE DESCRIPTION OF HEAVEN.
    A. Heaven Now.
    B. Heaven in Prospect.
  II. THE CONDITIONS IN HEAVEN.
    A. Activities in Heaven.
    B. Things Absent in Heaven.
    C. Things Present in Heaven.
  III. THE INHABITANTS OF HEAVEN.
    A. God.
    B. Angelic Beings.
    C. Elders.
    D. The Redeemed.
CONCLUSION.

References for Study:
    Ps. 99:1; Is. 6:1–7; Matt. 17:3; Luke 1:19,26; John 3:15; 4:24; 5:24; 10:28; 14:2; 17:2,24; Acts 7:48–56; Rom. 6:23; 8:18; 1 Cor. 6:2,3; 2 Cor. 5:6–8; 12:2–4; Eph. 1:10; Phil 1:23; Col. 1:15; 2 Tim. 2:12; Heb. 12:22,23; Rev. 4:2,3,10,11; 5:1–7,9,11; 7:9,10,15,16; 14:13; 15:3; 19:1,7,8; 20:10; 21:1–27; 22:1–5,17.

Memory Verse:
    And there shall be no night there; and they need no candle, neither light of the sun; for the Lord God giveth them light: and they shall reign for ever and ever (Rev. 22:5).

Aim:
    To teach the pupils what the Bible says about Heaven.

Point of Contact:
    Ask the students to help you plan an imaginary trip. It could be a trip to a well-known city such as New York or Los Angeles, or a visit to such a tourist attraction as Walt Disney World or Yellowstone National Park—whichever you prefer. Have the pupils describe, either on paper or verbally, some things they might expect to find at their destination. You may add to the student participation by obtaining posters or clipping pictures of this imaginary destination or by circling it on a map. Then remind your pupils that each of them will be given opportunity

to take a real, not an imaginary trip, to Heaven, and you are going to show them what to expect when they arrive.

INTRODUCTION.

The doctrines of Heaven and Hell are ignored, ridiculed, or denied by the world—and by much of the religious community. Listen to the comments of a world famous theologian and a scientist regarding Heaven: "It is unwise for Christians to claim any knowledge of either the furniture of heaven or the temperature of hell" (Dr. Reinhold Niebuhr). "As for Christian theology, can you imagine anything more appallingly idiotic than the Christian idea of heaven?" (Dr. Alfred Whitehead). But such ideas are not consistent with the Bible's account of Heaven, the hope and future home of the redeemed. For this reason we must impart to our students, simply and clearly, what the Bible actually says about that place called Heaven.

I. THE DESCRIPTION OF HEAVEN.

A. Heaven Now.

Much of what the Bible says about Heaven refers to a future time, a time after Christ has returned to earth, judged the world, and cast the wicked into the lake of fire. These events are described in the book of The Revelation, followed by a description, in Rev. 21–22, of God's great city, the New Jerusalem. We cannot say with absolute certainty whether the New Jerusalem now exists and is waiting to be fully revealed in those days following Christ's return, or whether it remains to be created. Many believe the New Jerusalem is already the location of God's throne. The Bible does not say for certain. But the Bible does tell us some very definite things about Heaven as it now exists. It is the abode of God and location of His throne (Rev. 4:2,3). Stephen preached this fact to the Jews and, through a supernatural vision, saw Christ there in Acts 7:48–56. Paul, in 2 Cor. 12:2–4, describes this heavenly place as paradise. Jesus, in John 14:2, assured the disciples that it was a place of dwelling and that He would personally prepare a place there for the redeemed. Since Jesus is at His Father's right hand in Heaven, then Heaven must also be the current dwelling place of those believers who have already died. We know this is true, because Paul twice assures us, in 2 Cor. 5:6–8 and Phil. 1:23, that the believer who departs this life goes into the presence of Christ.

B. Heaven in Prospect.

God gives us a beautiful and detailed description of the holy city called the New Jerusalem in Rev. 21—22. It is described as coming down from God and is called the bride or wife of the Lamb. This magnificent city will be square, according to Rev.

21:16, measuring 1,500 miles on each side. Its tallest point will be 1,500 miles high. The foundations of the city, described in Rev. 21:14,19,20, will be garnished with precious stones and will carry the names of the twelve apostles. Its walls, measuring 216 feet in height, will be made of jasper (Rev. 21:17,18). The city will have twelve gates, three on each side. Each gate, composed of a single pearl, will bear the name of one of the tribes of Israel (Rev. 21:12,13,21). The street of the city, mentioned in Rev. 21:21, will be of pure gold. According to Rev. 22:1-3, the throne of God and of the Lamb Christ Jesus will be in this holy city. Flowing out from that throne will be a crystal clear river of the water of life, and on either side will be planted the tree of life, bearing twelve types of fruit every month. This is the glorious city described as awaiting those whose names are written in the Lamb's book of life (Rev. 21:27).

II.   THE CONDITIONS IN HEAVEN.

Scripture repeatedly deals with conditions in Heaven. We have divided these into three groups: Activities, Things Absent, and Things Present.

A. Activities in Heaven.

The popular, but totally perverted, concept of Heaven pictures the future life in the skies in terms of disembodied spirits piously perched on fleecy clouds and strumming golden harps. This is not Bible truth. Heavenly activity, according to numerous references, will include singing, but will not be limited to singing (Rev. 5:9; 15:3). Our activity in Heaven, according to Rev. 7:15; 22:3, will also involve service. While we cannot be dogmatic on the exact nature of this service, we can conclude that a portion of our service will include exercising authority given by Christ. Study these passages: 2 Tim. 2:12; 1 Cor. 6:2,3; Rev. 22:5.

Heaven will also be a place of fellowship. During His transfiguration in Matt. 17:3, Jesus spoke freely with Moses and Elijah centuries after they had departed earth. Yet they were recognized as Moses and Elijah. In addition, the apostle John, during his vision of The Revelation, saw and recognized the difference between elders, angels, and various redeemed peoples. It seems logical that if recognition is possible, fellowship will also occur.

B. Things Absent in Heaven.

The Scriptures list several things that will be absent in Heaven. Rev. 7:16 tells us that there will be no more hunger, thirst, or excessive heat. Rev. 21 lists other things that will not be present: seas, vs. 1; tears, vs. 4; death, vs. 4; pain, vs. 4; sun or moon, vs. 23; night, vs. 25; and sin, vs. 27. The list continues in

Rev. 22:2 promising an end to the curse God placed upon the earth because of Adam's sin. Further, Satan will no longer be present to deceive men (Rev. 20:10).

C. Things Present in Heaven.

There are also things which we are promised will be present in Heaven. There will be glory (John 17:24; Rom. 8:18; Rev. 21:23); holiness (Rev. 21:27); divine light (Rev. 21:23–25; 22:5); unity (Eph. 1:10); and eternal life (John 3:15; 5:24; 10:28; 17:2; Rom. 6:23).

III. THE INHABITANTS OF HEAVEN.

Who will dwell in this holy city?

A. God.

All three persons of the Godhead will be present in Heaven. There seems to be no doubt that the one John sees sitting upon the throne in Rev. 4:2,3 is God the Father. Some question whether anyone could ever actually see a God who is spirit (John 4:24) and invisible (Col. 1:15). When John attempted to describe what he saw on that exalted throne, he could only write that the one who sat there was "like a jasper and a sardine stone." The Son will be there also, for in Rev. 5:1–7 we find the Lamb receiving the sealed book from the hand of Him who sits on the throne. He is in the midst of the throne, in the midst of heaven. He is the Lamb, the central personality of all history and in all Heaven. The Holy Spirit will be there also, depicted in Rev. 14:13; 22:17, as speaking to men on behalf of God.

B. Angelic Beings.

There are many references in the Old and New Testaments which teach the presence of angelic beings in Heaven (Heb. 12:22; Rev. 5:11; Is. 6:1–7; Ps. 99:1; Luke 1:19,26).

C. Elders.

John describes a group of twenty-four elders who are seated around God's throne in Rev. 4:4,10,11. Much has been written concerning the identity of these twenty-four elders. A reasonable suggestion is that they represent the twelve tribal leaders of Israel in the Old Testament and the twelve apostles of Jesus in the New Testament.

D. The Redeemed.

The writer of Hebrews tells us of a great assembly in Heaven in Heb. 12:23. John repeatedly mentions this great throng of people gathered from every nation and every people (Rev. 5:9; 7:9,10; 19:1,7,8). This great company will be those people whose sins have been washed away by the shed blood of the Lamb—Jesus Christ.

CONCLUSION.

The teacher should briefly review the description of Heaven and its conditions. Reviewing the list of those who will live in Heaven is a prime opportunity for evangelism. Not every lesson is basically evangelistic, but we should not teach a lesson on Heaven without taking advantage of the soul-winning opportunity it offers. Remind your pupils of the imaginary trip which opened the lesson and of the possibility of a trip to Heaven. Make sure they understand that they can make that trip, too, if they accept Christ as Saviour.

Reinforcing Illustrations:

1. Ask each student to imagine his favorite person or best friend. It may be a family member, a class mate, or a hero. Everyone enjoys being with his best friend. A creative teacher can tell a story of two friends and the things that they do together. There are two applications here. First, regardless of how wonderful our friends may be, Jesus is more wonderful. All the things we enjoy about our friends with be overshadowed by the Lord Himself. To be able to spend a great deal of time with a friend is good. To spend eternity with Jesus will be much better. Second, Christians can share eternity with earthly friends also, by telling them about Jesus and leading them to accept Him as Saviour.

2. Draw a circle on a chalkboard or poster. Ask the students to find the beginning and end of the circle. Just as we cannot find the end of a circle, we cannot find an end to Heaven. It will go on forever—eternally.

3. Ask one child to come to the front of the class. Tell him to begin running in place. Each time he stops—and he will stop—urge him to keep running. After he has been running for several minutes, ask him how he feels—tired, exhausted, out of breath. When he cannot, or will not, run any longer, bring him a chair. While he is seated, tell the class that the Bible compares life to running a race (Heb. 12:1) and that it promises a time of rest (Heb. 4:9). Heaven is a place where we, having finished our work on earth, will be at rest.

4. Following the Point of Contact theme of taking a trip, mimeograph tickets to Heaven. Write "Jesus" or appropriate Scripture references on the back of each ticket.

5. Using flash cards or a chalkboard, play a matching game with the following words:

Things Not in Heaven	Things in Heaven
Tears	Glory
Death	Holiness
Pain	Light
Night	Eternal Life
Sin	Angels
Unbelievers	God
	Christians

Scramble the words and have the students place them in the proper columns. Each student can place himself in the "Things in Heaven" column by accepting Jesus Christ.

Lesson Eleven: Heaven
Lesson Text: James 1:12
Craft: Heavenly Crown
Materials Needed:
Have crown fronts cut out in advance from yellow construction paper. These should have strips attached to make them long enough to fit around any of the children's heads.
Glue
Sequins, glitter, stars, etc.
Stapler

Instructions:
Give each child a crown to decorate. Supply him with glue, sequins, glitter, stars, etc. When decorated, fit the crown to each child's head, staple in place to fit, and let him wear the crown.

add extensions in same color to fit around the head

130

STUDY WORKSHEET

Lesson Eleven—HEAVEN

A DESCRIPTION OF HEAVEN.

1. Heaven is the abode of _____ and location of His _____ (Revelation 4:2,3).

2. Paul describes Heaven as a _____ in 2 Corinthians 12:2–4.

3. The Shape of Heaven is _____ (Revelation 21:16).

4. Heaven will have walls of _____, streets of _____ and gates of _____ (Revelation 21).

CONDITIONS OF HEAVEN.

1. Activities will include _____ (Revelation 5:9), and _____ (Revelation 22:5).

2. List four (4) things which will be absent in Heaven (Revelation 21:1–4).

   1.   3.

   2.   4.

3. List 3 things present in Heaven (Revelation 21).

   1.

   2.

   3.

4. Who will be in this holy city?

   1.   3.

   2.   4.

Memory Verse: And there shall be no night there; and they need no candle, neither light of the sun; for the Lord God giveth them light: and they shall reign for ever and ever (Revelation 22:5).

FOUNDATIONAL BIBLE DOCTRINES

Lesson Eleven—HEAVEN

A DESCRIPTION OF HEAVEN.

1. Heaven is the abode of **God** and location of His **throne** (Revelation 4:2,3).

2. Paul describes Heaven as a **paradise** in 2 Corinthians 12:2–4.

3. The Shape of Heaven is **square** (Revelation 21:16).

4. Heaven will have walls of **jasper**, streets of **gold** and gates of **pearl** (Revelation 21).

CONDITIONS OF HEAVEN.

1. Activities will include **singing** (Revelation 5:9), and **fellowship** (Revelation 22:5).

2. List four (4) things which will be absent in Heaven (Revelation 21:1–4).

   1. **hunger**   3. **death**
   2. **thirst**   4. **tears**

3. List 3 things present in Heaven (Revelation 21).

   1. **glory**
   2. **holiness**
   3. **unity**

4. Who will be in this holy city?

   1. **God**   3. **elders**
   2. **angels**   4. **the redeemed**

Memory Verse: And there shall be no night there; and they need no candle, neither light of the sun; for the Lord God giveth them light: and they shall reign for ever and ever (Revelation 22:5).

FOUNDATIONAL BIBLE DOCTRINES

Jerry Falwell, Pastor, Thomas Road Baptist Church
Lynchburg, Virginia

Lesson Twelve—Hell

INTRODUCTION.
I. THE DEFINITION OF HELL.
   A. Sheol.
   B. Hades.
   C. Gehenna.
II. THE LOCATION OF HELL.
III. THE NATURE OF HELL.
   A. Unquenchable Fire.
   B. Memory and Remorse.
   C. Thirst.
   D. Misery and Pain.
   E. Frustration and Anger.
   F. Separation.
   G. Divine Wrath.
   H. Prepared for Satan.
   I. Eternal.
IV. THE OCCUPANTS OF HELL.
   A. Satan.
   B. The Antichrist.
   C. The False Prophet.
   D. Fallen Angels.
   E. Judas Iscariot.
   F. All Unsaved People.
CONCLUSION.

References for Study:
Ex. 20:13; Num. 16:32,33; 2 Kgs. 23:10; 2 Chron. 28:1–4; Prov. 6:16–19; 29:25; Dan. 12:2; Hab. 3:2; Matt. 3:12; 8:1,2; 13:41,42; 22:13; 24:51; 25:30,41,46; Mark 9:43; Luke 16:19–31; John 3:16; 8:44; 9:22; 12:42,43; 14:2; Acts 1:25; Rom. 1:22,23; 16:20; Eph. 5:5; 2 Thes. 2:8; Heb. 13:4; 2 Pet. 2:4,17; 1 John 2:22; 3:15; Jude 6,7,13; Rev. 2:2,11; 9:21; 14:10; 18:23; 19:20; 20:6,10–15; 21:8.

Memory Verse:
And whosoever was not found written in the book of life was cast into the lake of fire (Rev. 20:15).

Aim:
To show the students the Bible reality of Hell, a place of eternal separation from God.

Point of Contact:
Discuss things that are opposite. Black is the opposite of white. Up is the opposite of down. Hot is the opposite of cold. Short is the opposite of tall. North is the opposite of South. There are thousands of examples. List several, asking the class to name the appropriate opposites. After several examples have been given, ask the class to give the opposite of righteous. The answer is, of course, unrighteous or wicked. (With younger students, use bad and good instead of righteous and unrighteous.) Explain that there is a place where only those people who have been made righteous through Jesus Christ can ever go—Heaven. Just as righteous has an opposite, so Heaven has an opposite—Hell.

INTRODUCTION.
Of all the many doctrines in the Bible, undoubtedly the very first that the unbeliever will deny and the weak believer will question is the doctrine of Hell! Satan has successfully accomplished this coveted goal through the following of three methods: (1) Rationalism, "There is no God, and therefore there can be no Hell;" (2) Ridicule, "There may be a God, but it is silly to speculate about multitudes of disembodied spirits flying in some literal lake of fire somewhere;" and (3) Religion, "There is a God, but He is a God of Love, and therefore would not and could not send anyone to Hell!" Regardless of the doubts and denials of men, the Bible dogmatically declares the existence and realty of Hell.

I.   THE DEFINITION OF HELL.
Here three key words must be defined:

A. Sheol.
Sheol is a Hebrew word, found sixty-five times in the Hebrew Old Testament. It is translated "hell" thirty-one times, "grave" thirty-one times, and "pit" three times.

B. Hades.
Hades is a Greek word, found eleven times in the Greek New Testament. It is translated "hell" in the King James Version. Both Sheol and Hades refer to the same place, but neither should be rendered "Hell." Many Bible students hold that Sheol-Hades was simply a temporary abode for all departed human spirits. It may have been divided into two compartments with a great gulf between them (Luke 16:26). The compartment for the saved in Hades (known as Paradise) was de-populated after the Cross by the Saviour Himself. The unsaved departed, however, continue to dwell in the fires of Hades awaiting their final judgment and destiny (Rev. 20:11–15).

C. Gehenna.

Gehenna is a Greek word (with a Hebrew background), found twelve times in the Greek New Testament and always translated correctly "Hell." A history of the word Gehenna will be helpful here. In the Old Testament, a wicked Israelite king named Ahaz forsook the worship of Jehovah and followed the devil-god Molech. In his insane and immoral attempt to please Molech, the king actually sacrificed his own children in the fires as burnt offerings to his abominable idol (2 Chron. 28:1–4). This all took place in a deep and narrow valley to the south of Jerusalem called the Valley of Hinnom. This terrible practice was stopped under the reign of godly king Josiah (2 Kgs. 23:10), but the Valley of Hinnom continued to be used as the dumping and burning ground for the garbage and filth of the city of Jerusalem. As one therefore combines both Old and New Testament meanings, he sees described a place of filth and sorrow, of smoke and pain, of fire and death! This, then, is the word the Holy Spirit chose to employ in describing the final destiny for the unsaved. With all these things in mind, one is forced to the sobering fact that Gehenna Hell is God's final dumping and burning place for the refuge of His universe—namely all unsaved men and apostate angels!

II.   THE LOCATION OF HELL.

Where is Gehenna Hell located? While the Bible definitely indicates that Hades is down in the heart of the earth somewhere (Num. 16:32,33), it teaches otherwise about Gehenna. It is described as "outer darkness," a place to which the unsaved are "cast" (Matt. 8:12; 22:13; 25:30). It is also described as a "mist of darkness" (2 Pet. 2:17) and as the "blackness of darkness" (Jude 13). From these verses it becomes immediately clear that Gehenna Hell may well be located away from this earth, a place of outer darkness, to be found perhaps in some remote spot near the edge of God's universe.

If one thus distinguishes between Hades Hell and Gehenna Hell, he will understand the words of John in describing the final resurrection of the wicked dead and their judgment. John writes: "And death and hell were cast into the lake of fire . . ." (Rev. 20:14). By this John meant that both death (which claimed the bodies of all dead unbelievers) and hell (that is, Hades Hell, which had held the spirits of all unsaved men) gave up their possessions, thus resulting in the joined bodies and spirits of all the unsaved being cast into Gehenna Hell!

III.   THE NATURE AND CHARACTERISTICS OF HELL.

What will Gehenna really be like? Consider these characteristics:

A. Unquenchable Fire.

Hell is a place of unquenchable fire (Matt. 3:12; 13:41,42; Mark 9:43).

B. Memory and Remorse.

Hell is a place of memory and remorse. In Luke 16:19–31 the unsaved rich man experienced memory and remorse over his lost condition in Hades. Surely these experiences will not be lessened in Gehenna.

C. Thirst.

Hell is a place of thirst. Again in the Luke 16 account we read of the rich man's plea for a drop of water to cool his tongue (Luke 16:24).

D. Misery and Pain.

Hell is a place of misery and pain (Rev. 14:10,11).

E. Frustration and Anger.

Hell is a place of frustration and anger (Matt. 13:42; 24:51).

F. Separation.

Hell is a place of separation. Often the unsaved man jokes about Hell in the following manner: "Well, if I do go to Hell, I won't be lonely, for all my friends will be there too." But quite the opposite is true. In at least four separate passages (Rev. 2:11; 20:6,14; 21:8) Gehenna Hell is called "the second death." Death in the Bible refers to separation. Thus Hell is literally the second death, for the sinner will be forever separated from God. And, inasmuch as Gehenna is a place of darkness, this separation will doubtless isolate him from the companionship of unsaved friends as well.

G. Divine Wrath.

Hell is a place of undiluted divine wrath. Man has already experienced some of God's wrath on this earth, though not in its pure state. After the flood there has been the rainbow, for up to this point God has always heard and answered the prophet Habakkuk's prayer, "O Lord . . . in wrath remember mercy" (Hab. 3:2). But no more! All living unsaved men should carefully ponder over the following frightful words: "The same shall drink of the wine of the wrath of God, which is poured out without mixture into the cup of his indignation . . ." (Rev. 14:10). God's final wrath will not be mixed with mercy.

H. Prepared for Satan.

Hell is a place originally prepared for Satan and his hosts. Perhaps the saddest fact about Hell is that unsaved man goes there as an uninvited guest: "Then shall he say . . . Depart from me, ye cursed, into everlasting fire, prepared for the devil and his angels" (Matt. 25:41). How tragic therefore when the sinner will refuse Heaven, that place prepared for all repenting men (John 14:2), only to eventually descend into Hell, a place originally not created for him!

I. Eternal.

Hell is a place created for all eternity. The Greek word for everlasting is aionios (eye-o-nee-as), and is found seventy-one times in the New Testament. Sixty-four of these instances are in reference to God, such as His eternal power, spirit, kingdom, covenant, etc. The remaining seven instances are directly related to the duration of Hell. In other words, Hell will continue as long as God's works continue, which is forever (Dan. 12:2; Matt. 25:46; Jude 7).

IV.   THE OCCUPANTS OF HELL.

Who shall be someday confined to Gehenna forever?

A. Satan.

"And the God of peace shall bruise Satan under your feet shortly" (Rom. 16:20). "And the devil that deceived them was cast into the lake of fire and brimstone . . ." (Rev. 20:10).

B. The Antichrist.

"And then shall that Wicked [one] be revealed, whom the Lord shall consume with the spirit of his mouth, and shall destroy with the brightness of his coming" (2 Thes. 2:8).

C. The False Prophet.

"And the beast [Antichrist] was taken, and with him the false prophet that wrought miracles before him . . . These both were cast alive into a lake of fire burning with brimstone" (Rev. 19:20). As this judgment takes place prior to the millennium, these two foul criminals thus become the first and second unsaved creatures to enter the lake of fire!

D. Fallen Angels.

"For if God spared not the angels that sinned, but cast them down to hell, and delivered them into chains of darkness, to be reserved unto judgment" (2 Pet. 2:4). The word translated Hell is "Tartaros" in the Greek New Testament and is found only here. It is possible that Tartaros is a special place in Gehenna. "And the angels which kept not their first estate, but left their own habitation, he hath reserved in everlasting chains under darkness unto the judgment of the great day" (Jude 6).

E. Judas Iscariot.

The betrayer of Jesus Christ is singled out here in particular because there are those (notably the late Kenneth S. Wuest of the Moody Bible Institute faculty) who believe Judas will be consigned to a special place in Gehenna on the basis of Peter's words concerning Judas in the upper room just prior to Pentecost: "Judas by transgression fell, that he might go to his own place" (Acts 1:25).

F. All Unsaved People.

In Rev. 21:8 John classifies all sinners into eight general categories. These are: the fearful (Prov. 29:25; John 9:22; John 12:42,43); the unbelieving (John 3:16); the abominable (Prov. 6:16–19); murderers (Ex. 20:13; 1 John 3:15); whoremongers (Eph. 5:5; Heb. 13:4); sorcerers (Rev. 9:21; 18:23); idolaters (Rom. 1:22,23); and liars (John 8:44; 1 John 2:22; Rev. 2:2).

CONCLUSION.

Hell is a reality. It is a place of unspeakable torment. It is eternal. There is no escape from it except through Christ. The teacher should use this lesson to reach any unsaved students and to challenge saved students to actively win souls to Christ.

Reinforcing Illustrations:

Nearly all the illustrations provided for the lesson on Heaven can be used with this lesson—in reverse.

1. Separation is the overwhelming characteristic of Hell. Hell means separation from a God of love and from Jesus, our best friend. Those in Hell will be separated forever from Christian friends. Hell's blackness will separate them even from other men and women and boys and girls who spend eternity in that awful place. Likewise, Christians need to be reminded that unless they carry the gospel to their family and friends, Hell will separate them forever from those whom they love. The teacher would be wise to remind the students of last week's story of two friends together and how Hell could be an unhappy ending to even the best of stories.

2. The circle can be used just as effectively to illustrate the eternity of Hell as it was used to show the eternity of Heaven.

3. Review last week's word game. Now add a third column:

Things in
Hell

Thirst
Fire
Satan
Fallen angels
Judas

Point out that everything from last week's "Things Not in Heaven" column will also be in Hell—including everyone who does not accept Jesus Christ.

Lesson Twelve: Hell
Lesson Text: Rev. 20:15
Craft: Finger Painting
Materials Needed:
 Finger paint in orange, yellow, red
 White butcher or finger paint paper
 Shirts or aprons (each child could bring one of his father's old shirts—provide extras for those who forget.)

Instructions:
After a lesson in which Hell is discussed, allow the children to finger paint a picture of fire.

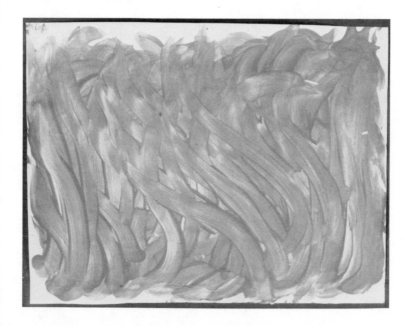

STUDY WORKSHEET

Lesson Twelve—HELL

THREE NAMES OF HELL ARE:

1. _____

2. _____

3. _____

Hell is a place of _____ (Matthew 8:12).

NATURE AND CHARACTERISTICS OF HELL.

1. The fire of Hell is _____ (Matthew 3:12).

2. The unsaved rich man experienced _____ and _____ in Hell (Luke 16:19–31).

3. The rich man wanted a drop of _____ to cool his tongue (Luke 16:24).

4. Death in the Bible refers to _____.

5. Other characteristics of Hell are: _____, _____, _____, and _____.

OCCUPANTS OF HELL.

1. Hell was prepared for _____ and his _____ (Matthew 25:41).

2. Other occupants of Hell will be _____, _____, _____, and all the _____ (Revelation 21:8).

Memory Verse: And whosoever was not found written in the book of life was cast into the lake of fire (Revelation 20:15).

FOUNDATIONAL BIBLE DOCTRINES

Lesson Twelve—HELL

THREE NAMES OF HELL ARE:

1. **Sheol**
2. **Hades**
3. **Gehenna**

Hell is a place of **outer darkness** (Matthew 8:12).

NATURE AND CHARACTERISTICS OF HELL.

1. The fire of Hell is **unquenchable** (Matthew 3:12).
2. The unsaved rich man experienced **memory** and **remorse** in Hell (Luke 16:19–31).
3. The rich man wanted a drop of **water** to cool his tongue (Luke 16:24).
4. Death in the Bible refers to **separation**.
5. Other characteristics of Hell are: **wrath**, **eternal**, **frustration**, and **anger**.

OCCUPANTS OF HELL.

1. Hell was prepared for **Satan** and his **angels** (Matthew 25:41).
2. Other occupants of Hell will be **the Antichrist**, **false prophet**, **fallen angels**, and all the **unsaved** (Revelation 21:8).

Memory Verse: And whosoever was not found written in the book of life was cast into the lake of fire (Revelation 20:15).

FOUNDATIONAL BIBLE DOCTRINES

Jack Hyles, Pastor, First Baptist Church
Hammond, Indiana

Lesson Thirteen—The Second Coming of Christ

INTRODUCTION.
  I. THE TRUTH OF HIS COMING.
    A. He Is Coming Again.
    B. He Will Return Just as He Went Away.
    C. His Coming Will Be Visible.
    D. His Coming is Imminent.
 II. THE ORDER OF EVENTS AT HIS COMING.
    A. The Lord Will Descend from Heaven.
    B. He Will Come with a Shout.
    C. He Will Come with the Voice of the Archangel.
    D. He Will Come with the Sound of a Trumpet.
    E. The Dead in Christ Shall Rise.
    F. The Living Saved Shall Be Caught Up.
III. OUR BEHAVIOR IN VIEW OF HIS COMING.
    A. We Should Be Comforted by His Coming.
    B. We Should Look for His Coming.
    C. We Should Live Clean Lives Awaiting His Coming.
    D. We Should Be Blessed by His Coming.
    E. We Should Speak about His Coming.
    F. We Should Love His Coming.
    G. We Should Be Faithful to Church Attendance.
CONCLUSION.

References for Study:
   Luke 15:7,10; John 14:1–3; Acts 1:10,11; 1 Cor. 13:12; 2 Cor. 5:10; Phil 1:23; 1 Thes. 4:13–18; 2 Tim. 4:8; Tit. 2:13–15; Heb. 9:28; 10:25; 12:1; John 3:2,3; Rev. 1:3,7; 19:7–9,11–14; 20:1–6,11–15; 21; 22.

Memory Verse:
   And if I go and prepare a place for you, I will come again, and receive you unto myself, that where I am, there ye may be also (John 14:3).

Aim:
   To teach my pupils the truth of the doctrine of our Lord's return and to teach them to prepare for His return.

Point of Contact:
   There is a little outline we should learn concerning the return of Jesus:

147

1. He came TO His own. (In Bethlehem)
2. He is coming FOR His own. (At the Rapture)
3. He is coming WITH His own. (After the 7-year tribulation)

The teacher should have the pupils repeat this outline over and over again, explaining to them that in Bethlehem Jesus came TO His own; at any time He is going to come FOR His own, calling us out of the world into the air for the Marriage of the Lamb and the Judgment Seat of Christ, where we will be for seven years; then at the end of that seven years, we will come back to earth with Him when He comes WITH His own.

INTRODUCTION.

The teacher could go to the blackboard and chart the course of both the believer and unbeliever concerning their future as follows:

The believer lives on earth until his death. At death his body goes to the grave and his spirit goes to be with Jesus (Phil. 1:23). This means he goes to Heaven. Though he does not have his final glorified body, nevertheless, he does have a body and will stay in Heaven until the resurrection of the just. There in Heaven he can see and witness what transpires on earth (Luke 15:7,10; Heb. 12:1). He knows people in Heaven and is known in Heaven as he was known on earth (1 Cor. 13:12). He stays in Heaven until the first resurrection (the Rapture) when his body rises from the grave and his spirit descends from Heaven. The spirit reenters the body, and the spirit and body will be with Jesus in the air (1 Thes. 4:13–17). That body will be like Jesus' body (1 John 3:2). It will be flesh and bone and will be recognizable. While in the air for seven years, the Christian appears before the Judgment Seat of Christ to receive rewards, and he participates in the Marriage of the Lamb (2 Cor. 5:10; Rev. 19:7–9). The Christian is in the air for seven years. During that seven-year period a time of terrible tribulation is in progress on the earth, at the end of which the Christian comes back to earth with Jesus (Rev. 19:11–14). He then rules and reigns with Christ on the earth for 1000 years (Rev. 20:1–6). At the end of this 1000-year period, he enters into the New Jerusalem, where he will live forever with Christ (Rev. 21—22).

The unsaved man lives on earth until he dies, when his body goes to the grave. At death, his soul goes to Hades, a place of fire and torment. The soul of the unsaved man continues at this place while the Christian is being resurrected at the Rapture, throughout the Marriage of the Lamb, the Judgment Seat of Christ, the Tribulation Period and the Millennium. At the end of the Millennium, the body of the unsaved man rises and both body and soul stand before God at the Great White Throne Judgment (Rev. 20:11–15). There he receives his degrees of punishment and body and soul are cast into Hell forever.

Now for the lesson let us single out that part which we call the Rapture. It is the first step of two steps concerning our Lord's return. It is a time when He comes FOR His own.

I. THE TRUTH OF HIS COMING.
A. He Is Coming Again.
This is a personal promise which Jesus Himself gave to His disciples (John 14:1–3).

B. He Will Return Just as He Went Away.
This means that He will return both bodily and physically (Acts 1:10,11).

C. His Coming Will Be Visible.
Every eye shall see Him (Rev. 1:7).

D. His Coming is Imminent.
Read 1 Thes. 4:15. Notice the word "we" in verse 15. Paul was expecting Him to come in his lifetime. In Rev. 1:3 we find "the time is at hand." In other words, Jesus could have come at any time from His going until now, and could come at any time in the future. This means His coming is imminent.

II. THE ORDER OF EVENTS AT HIS COMING.
A. The Lord Will Descend from Heaven.

B. He Will Come with a Shout.
This, of course, is the victor's shout.

C. He Will Come with the Voice of the Archangel.

D. He Will Come with the Sound of a Trumpet.
The trumpet in Bible times was used for several things.
1. For a special gathering to a feast.
2. As a battle cry.
3. At a time of reunion.
So shall the coming of our Lord be a time of a wonderful feast, a time to defeat Satan, and a time to be reunited with Christ and all of our loved ones who died in Him.

E. The Dead in Christ Shall Rise.
All of those who have died in Christ will be raised from the dead, and their spirits shall reinhabit their bodies.

F. The Living Saved Shall Be Changed and Caught Up to Meet the Lord in the Air with Those Who are Being Resurrected.

III. OUR BEHAVIOR IN VIEW OF HIS COMING.

A. We Should Be Comforted by His Coming.
When the Christian goes to the graveside, he may be comforted by this great truth (1 Thes. 4:18). When the Christian is ill, he can be comforted by this great truth. When the Christian faces death, he may be comforted by this great truth.

B. We Should Look for His Coming.
Read Heb. 9:28. The word "look" here means "gaze." We should constantly be gazing toward the sky awaiting His return.

C. We Should Live Clean Lives Awaiting His Coming.
The Christian should not do anything that he would not be pleased to be doing at the return of his Lord (1 John 3:2,3). (Teacher, go through some things here that the pupils would be ashamed to be doing at our Lord's return.)

D. We Should Be Blessed by His Coming.
Read Tit. 2:13. You will notice His return is called the blessed hope. We should anticipate His coming and be blessed at the thought of it.

E. We Should Speak about His Coming.
Tit. 2:13–15.

F. We Should Love His Coming.
2 Tim. 4:8.

G. We Should Be Faithful to Church Attendance Because of His Coming.
Heb. 10:25.

CONCLUSION.
There will be tragedy at His coming. The pupils should be reminded concerning what will transpire on earth at His coming. Draw on their imagination for a few minutes as they consider what will happen to automobiles driven by Christians at the Rapture, trains conducted by Christians, airplanes flown by Christians. We should not forget the tragedy of people looking for their loved ones, babies missing, husbands gone, wives gone. Lead them to realize and imagine what it would be like on earth when all the Christians are gone. Think of the plane crashes, the train wrecks, the automobile accidents, etc.

Reinforcing Illustrations:
1. The teacher could bring a magnet to class along with some wood shavings and metal shavings. He could mix the metal and wood shavings together and hold the magnet over them. Of

course, the metal shavings will rise to meet the magnet. This is a picture of our Lord's return. Jesus is the magnet; the metal shavings are His people; the wooden shavings are those who are not His people.

2. Notice the attached chart. Go through the chart with the pupils. Draw it on the blackboard; then erase it. Have a pupil come to the blackboard and draw the same chart.

3. The teacher could bring several objects to class, or if the objects are unavailable, he could bring pictures of these objects to class: a trumpet, a crown, an angel, a tombstone, an empty car, etc. Point to the objects and ask the pupils to tell what these objects have to do with the coming of Christ.

4. The lesson could actually be acted out. Lying on the floor could represent death; standing on a chair could represent being in the air. The pupils could actually act out the future of the Christian and the future of the unsaved.

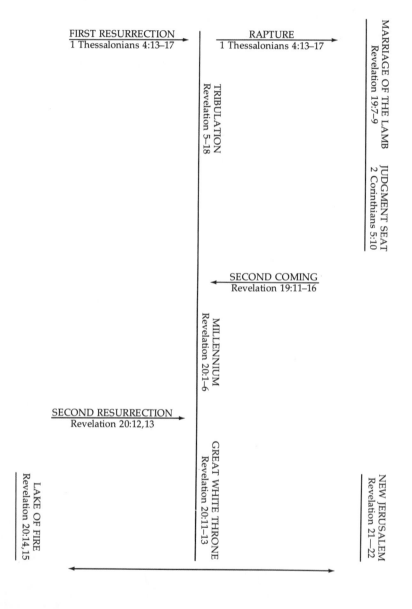

—*THE FUTURE OF THE SAVED AND UNSAVED*—
(ORDER OF EVENTS)

FIRST RESURRECTION
1 Thessalonians 4:13–17

RAPTURE
1 Thessalonians 4:13–17

MARRIAGE OF THE LAMB
Revelation 19:7–9

TRIBULATION
Revelation 5–18

JUDGMENT SEAT
2 Corinthians 5:10

SECOND COMING
Revelation 19:11–16

MILLENNIUM
Revelation 20:1–6

SECOND RESURRECTION
Revelation 20:12,13

GREAT WHITE THRONE
Revelation 20:11–13

NEW JERUSALEM
Revelation 21—22

LAKE OF FIRE
Revelation 20:14,15

152

Lesson Thirteen: The Second Coming
Lesson Text: 1 Thes. 4:16
Craft: Trumpet and Cloud Mobile

Materials Needed:

Thread or twine—cut in 10-12" pieces (any color), seven per child

Sticks—three per child. These can be cut from plastic straws, popsicle sticks, or twigs can be used. These should be approximately 6" and 10" but do not have to be of an exact length. Longer sticks should be used for the center top.

Shapes—Four of each per child: clouds—cut from white construction paper. Trumpets—cut from gold or yellow construction paper.

(Shapes should be cut from the same pattern so that they can be glued back to back.)

Instructions:

A model mobile should be prepared and hung in the classroom during this exercise. Children should be seated at tables and each child should be given three sticks. One piece of thread can be pre-tied to the middle of each stick to speed the time necessary for completion. Table teachers should assist each child as they tie the strings from the two lower sticks to the upper sticks. Two strings should then be tied to either end of the lower sticks, and the shapes glued to the end of these strings so that the string is caught and glued between two of the same shapes. Once the mobile is completely together, the mobile should be held up and the string positioned on the sticks and adjusted until none ofhthe shapes hit each other when allowed to hang freely. Strings should then be secured in place with glue.

glue string here

glue string here

cut 4 of each shape for
each child

STUDY WORKSHEET

Lesson Thirteen—THE SECOND COMING OF CHRIST

THE TRUTH OF HIS COMING.

1. Jesus said, "I will come _____" (John 14:1–3).

2. He will return _____ and _____ (Acts 1:10,11).

3. When He comes, every _____ shall see Him (Revelation 1:7).

4. His Coming is _____, which means at any time (Revelation 1:3).

THE ORDER OF EVENTS.

1. Christ will _____ from Heaven with a _____ with the voice of the _____.

2. At the sound of a _____ the _____ in Christ will rise, followed by the _____ saved (1 Thessalonians 4:16,17).

OUR BEHAVIOR IN VIEW OF HIS COMING.

1. We can _____ one another with the promise of Christ's return (1 Thessalonians 4:18).

2. Because we are _____ for this blessed hope we are to _____ ourselves (1 John 3:3; Titus 2:13).

Memory Verse: And if I go and prepare a place for you, I will come again, and receive you unto myself; that where I am, there ye may be also (John 14:3).

FOUNDATIONAL BIBLE DOCTRINES

Lesson Thirteen—THE SECOND COMING OF CHRIST

THE TRUTH OF HIS COMING.

1. Jesus said, "I will come **again**" (John 14:1–3).
2. He will return **bodily** and **physically** (Acts 1:10,11).
3. When He comes, every **eye** shall see Him (Revelation 1:7).
4. His Coming is **imminent**, which means at any time (Revelation 1:3).

THE ORDER OF EVENTS.

1. Christ will **descend** from Heaven with a **shout** with the voice of the **archangel**.
2. At the sound of a **trumpet** the **dead** in Christ will rise, followed by the **living** saved (1 Thessalonians 4:16,17).

OUR BEHAVIOR IN VIEW OF HIS COMING.

1. We can **comfort** one another with the promise of Christ's return (1 Thessalonians 4:18).
2. Because we are **looking** for this blessed hope, we are to **purify** ourselves (1 John 3:3; Titus 2:13).

Memory Verse: And if I go and prepare a place for you, I will come again, and receive you unto myself, that where I am, there ye may be also (John 14:3).